Political Writings of William Morris

LAWRENCE & WISHART LTD. LONDON

Political Writings
of
William Morris

EDITOR: A. L. MORTON

BY THE EDITOR

A People's History of England
Language of Men
The English Utopia
Socialism in Britain
The Matter of Britain
The Life and Ideas of Robert Owen
The World of the Ranters

Freedom in Arms
A Selection of Leveller Writings

With George Tate
The British Labour Movement,
1770—1920

Political Writings of William Morris

Edited and with an Introduction by
A. L. MORTON

1979

LAWRENCE AND WISHART LONDON

This edition is published simultaneously by
Lawrence & Wishart, London, International Publishers,
New York, and Seven Seas Books, Berlin, 1973
Second impression by Lawrence
& Wishart and International Publishers, 1979
SBN 85315-257-8

CONTENTS

FOREWORD

IN making my selections for this volume I have given "political" the widest possible interpretation. It is impossible to draw a hard and fast line between what Morris wrote about art and what he wrote about politics. Any attempt to do so would be to distort his whole outlook and teaching. I have tried to give as wide a view as is possible within the scope of a single volume of the range and variety of his work. The items are given in chronological order so as to make it possible to follow the development of his thought. All are given in full, except that a few lines dealing with family matters have been omitted from the letters to Jane Morris.

Each item is prefaced with a short note giving information about bibliographical and other matters, but I have made no attempt at a full bibliography. For a number of details I am indebted to the invaluable appendices to Professor Eugene D. Lemire's *The Unpublished Lectures of William Morris*. In these notes I have used the following abbreviations:

Collected Works—The Collected Works of William Morris, ed. May Morris.

May Morris—*William Morris: Artist, Writer, Socialist*, ed. May Morris.

Cole—*William Morris: Selected Writings*, ed. G. D. H. Cole.

Jackson—*William Morris on Art and Socialism*, ed. Holbrook Jackson.

The bulk of the volume is drawn from Morris' lectures. These were prepared by him with very great care and fully written out before delivery. Many of them were repeated on a number of occasions and his daughter May gives us an entertaining description of the consequences to the manuscripts:

"The very MS of it is eloquent: the stout hand-made paper with ragged torn edges, notes of questions to the lecturer decorated with pretty branch-work in the back of one or two pages, these leaves of foolscap have been many a journey through the London working-men's clubs and around the industrial cities of England and Scotland. They also talk to you and say, 'Look, we are part of a batch of paper this man used for his poetry, writing at leisure in his study, and we went to the printers all clean and respectable and self-satisfied: now we are used for this strange new talk and . . . we are rushed about the country in that familiar brown haversack of his, and sometimes handed to a reporter to look at, and we get raggeder every week—a hard life; we are old and worn before our time—actually frilled at the edges'."

Like his manuscripts, Morris himself was "worn before his time" in his devotion to the cause of Socialism.

INTRODUCTION

IT may seem an odd way of introducing a volume of theoretical writings to say that their author was little of a political theorist, yet this was the truth about William Morris. As he put it himself, his mind was constructive rather than analytical. And we can say, to round off the paradox, that this was his greatest strength, the reason why his political thoughts are, if anything, truer and more apposite today than when they were written nearly a century ago. As Edward Thompson says: "Unsteady among generalisations, weak in analytic thought, his response to life was immediate and concrete."[1] He did not think easily, but he thought deeply and what he thought was always his own, the outcome of life, of experience.

The result was that when, quite late in life, he came to Socialism he came already rich, with a background ready to take the ideas of Socialism (which for him were always the ideas of Marxism) and build them into a mature and well founded fabric. Socialism was not a denial or a reversal of his earlier life and thinking, but a fulfilment and an enlarging. For this reason his political writings need to be understood in the light of his whole background and development.

THE ROAD TO SOCIALISM

Morris was born in 1834 into a family that was already well-to-do and was soon to become rich by the standards of Victorian England. He had a sheltered childhood and was sent to school at Marlborough, which, fortunately for him, was then new and poorly organised. Consequently he enjoyed a good deal of freedom which he liked to spend

1 Edward P. Thompson: *William Morris, Romantic to Revolutionary*, p. 834.

exploring the surrounding countryside—exceptionally rich in the monuments of man's past. One of his earliest letters records a visit to Silbury Mount and the great stone circle at Avebury, which, characteristically, he not only enjoyed but measured and examined carefully. At Oxford, to which he went in 1853, the past was even more powerfully present.

The High Church Oxford Movement, which was still attracting serious-minded students, appealed to his sense of history and drew his attention to the life and art of the Middle Ages. Carlyle and Ruskin at first supplemented and soon replaced and redirected this interest. These years of the middle eighty-fifties were a time when Victorian capitalism seemed most secure and invincible. The challenge of Chartism had been defeated, after 1848 the danger of revolt in Europe seemed ended. No serious rival to British industrial supremacy had yet appeared anywhere in the world. In Britain itself the hideous and deadly squalor of the new factory towns was perhaps at its worst—still untouched by more than the barest beginnings of planning or sanitation.

In these circumstances Morris' romantic medievalism was a challenge to the ethic and values dominating society. Nor was he alone. At Oxford he found friends like Edward Burne-Jones and Cormell Price who shared his feelings and had considerably more experience of actual social conditions. At first this revolt took vague and idealistic forms. They planned, as Burne-Jones wrote, a "Crusade and Holy Warfare against the Age." And, as yet, his opposition was artistic rather than political. In a letter to Price in July 1856 Morris said:

"I can't enter into politico-social subjects with any interest, for on the whole I see that things are in a muddle, and I have no power or vocation to set them right in ever so little a degree. My work is the embodiment of dreams in one form or another."[2]

2 *Letters of William Morris*. Ed. Philip Henderson, p. 17.

In this hour of triumphant capitalism the few who rejected it felt helpless and isolated—it was hard to see how the enemy could be defeated or even how one could come to grips with him. Morris, for all his talk about dreams, was essentially practical and combative and the next part of his life was taken up with the search for a satisfactory battleground.

By the time this letter was written he had abandoned his original idea of becoming a clergyman and had begun to work in an architect's office. Soon he met Rossetti and abandoned architecture intending to become an artist. This, in a sense, was a false step. Morris had gifts that would have made him a fine architect—as a painter he could never have been more than mediocre, as he soon discovered. But behind his abandonment of architecture there lay perhaps an important positive development. He and his friends at Oxford were influenced by the Gothic revival which was soon to cover England with Early English churches and Perpendicular town halls. Even worse, the fashion for "restoring" ancient buildings was leading to their whole-sale destruction.

Under the influence of Ruskin Morris was soon able to see the fallacy behind this sham gothicism. The true Gothic of the Middle Ages was the work of craftsmen, of men who did their own thinking, whose hand and brain formed a unity, who were, therefore, in a very real sense, free. In one of his earlier lectures, *The Art of the People,* he said:

"Those treasures of architecture that we study so care-fully nowadays—what are they? how were they made? ... who was it that designed and ornamented them? The great architect, carefully kept for the purpose, and guarded from the common troubles of common men? By no means. Sometimes, perhaps, it was the monk, the ploughman's brother; oftenest his other brother, the village carpenter, smith, mason, what not—'a common fellow', whose com-mon everyday labour fashioned works that are to-day the wonder and despair of many a hard-working 'cultivated' architect. And did he loathe his work? No, it is impossible. I have seen, as most of us have, work done by such men in some out-of-the-way hamlet—where to-day, even, few strangers ever come, and whose people seldom go five miles from their own doors; in such places, I say, I have seen work so delicate, so careful, and so inventive, that nothing in its way could go further. And I will assert, without fear of contradiction, that no human ingenuity can produce such work as this without pleasure being a third party to the brain that conceived and the hand that fashioned it."

Morris is saying that while modern technique can imitate old forms the life behind them comes from the whole man, totally engaged in what he is doing. Such work cannot be reproduced by the wage earner under capitalism who is required to be no more than a hand.

It was this conviction which led Morris in the end from artistic criticism to social criticism and from social criticism to political action. He came to think that while capitalism exploits the worker economically by the extraction of surplus value it exploits him no less grievously by robbing him of his humanity, of work which he could enjoy and which calls out all his powers of hand and brain. Morris never used the term alienation and the writings of Marx on the subject were unpublished and unknown in his time. Yet, starting from his own particular standpoint, Morris reached a position pretty well identical with what we know now, though he could not have known it then, had been earlier developed by Marx. It may well be that the most important single aspect of the work to be found in this volume is his stress upon the positive value of labour in man's development.

With his views Morris could hardly have been happy in the field of architecture as it was practised in Victorian England, where, as he wrote, it

"could do nothing but produce on the one hand pedantic imitations of classical architecture of the most revolting ugliness, and ridiculous travesties of Gothic buildings, not quite so ugly, but meaner and sillier; and, on the other hand, the utilitarian brick box with a slate lid which the Anglo-Saxon generally in modern times considers a good sensible house with no nonsense about it."

Nevertheless his architectural studies played an important part in his development and were later to be of considerable use to him.

At this stage he and the Pre-Raphaelites in general were engaged in a movement of protest, not against capitalism as a system of exploitation but against industrialism as a creator of squalor and ugliness. This was as far as most of them ever got: for Morris it was a starting point from which he advanced steadily. Meanwhile, in 1857, they were all happily engaged in decorating the new Union buildings in Oxford with murals from Malory's *Morte d'Arthur,* and Morris met and married Jane Burden. Marriage brought new problems and a new step forward. He found that if he wanted a house he could be happy in he must build it himself, the result being the Red House at Bexley Heath, which, incidentally, was an important event in the history of English domestic architecture. And having built his house he found nothing he could bear to put in it. Capitalism, he discovered, produced only ugly, pretentious luxury goods for slave owners and ugly shoddy goods for slaves. He therefore set to work to furnish his house with things that were honest in substance and workmanship and good in design. Out of this grew the famous Morris firm, setting new standards which have affected every aspect of furniture and interior decoration. As he said long afterwards to a *Clarion* interviewer:

"I have tried to produce goods which should be genuine so far as their mere substances are concerned, and should have on that account the primary beauty in them which belongs to naturally treated natural substances; have tried for instance to make woollen substances as woollen as possible, cotton as cotton as possible, and so on; have used only the dyes which are natural and simple."

"The Firm" produced high quality furniture, textiles, wallpapers, carpets and other goods, and gave Morris a national reputation in the world of design and craftsmanship. Yet it left him unsatisfied. Since all his goods had to be of the highest standard they were necessarily expensive, and he grew increasingly impatient at his role of purveyor of beautiful things for the rich. If this was part of the "war against the Age" it was no more than a skirmish of outposts.

This was only one of a number of activities that were making him an important public figure. Between 1867 and 1877 he published several volumes of poetry, of which *The Life and Death of Jason, The Earthly Paradise* and *Sigurd the Volsung* are the best known. All these are long narrative poems looking back to times when life seemed simpler and more heroic, and to this extent they also may be regarded as a part of the "war against the Age". In fact they were (and to an extent still are) regarded rather as agreeably escapist costume pieces, though their technical dexterity gave him a respectable place among nineteenth century poets. This assessment was hardly fair to Morris, though I think poetry came too easily to him for him ever to reach the greatest heights.

A third public reputation was made by his foundation and leadership of the Society for the Protection of Ancient Buildings (popularly known as "Anti-Scrape") whose object was

"to keep a watch on old monuments, to protest against all 'restoration' that means more than keeping out wind and weather . . . and to awake a feeling that our ancient buildings are not mere ecclesiastical toys, but sacred monuments of the nation's growth and hope."

Thus, in his early forties, Morris was a distinguished figure, yet, at each stage, his inner development outgrew his success and every new achievement left him the more unsatisfied as he saw how much more he had been unable to do. Quite early he was asking himself what was wrong with the basis of a society which could produce so much ugliness and whose arts were, as he saw, in so unhealthy a condition. It came down to a conviction that the trouble was the lack of freedom in the modern world. But what was freedom? This was something that a man of his temperament could learn best, perhaps only, from the consideration of actual cases. He had long been attracted by the history and literature of the heroic age of the European North. As he wrote to Andreas Scheu:

"The delightful freshness and independence of thought of them [the Sagas], the air of freedom which breathes through them, their worship of courage (the great virtue of the human race), their utter unconventionality took my heart by storm."[3]

He was perhaps too ready to overlook some of the less attractive sides of this way of life.

Most of all he was drawn to what he knew of ancient Iceland, and his visit to that country in 1871 was perhaps a decisive turning point in his life. Iceland, he saw, was an exceptionally free country because of the high degree of equality of condition prevailing there. By this phrase Morris, like most of the early English Socialists, meant simply the absence of classes and class exploitation. In the same letter to Scheu he wrote:

"I went to Iceland and ... I learned one lesson there, thoroughly I hope, that the most grinding poverty is a trifling evil compared with the inequality of classes."

Once this had been learnt the way to Socialism lay open before him: when he encountered the ideas of Marx he had no difficulty in recognising that they were really a more precise and scientific expression of what he had long known in his heart.

3 Henderson, op. cit., p. 186.

He had one more lesson to master before his apprenticeship was complete. Living in extremely comfortable circumstances he had as yet no contact with the working class and no experience of political activity. Both came with his involvement from 1876 to 1878 in the struggle against the threat by Disraeli's Tory government to plunge Britain into a war with Russia in order to preserve the rule of Turkey in the Balkans. Perhaps there were complexities here which he did not entirely understand, but what he saw he saw clearly and expressed in a manifesto addressed to "the Working men of England."

The Tory government, he declared, was dragging England into an unjust war to maintain its imperial position in India and the interests of the holders of Turkish Bonds. Its supporters were "greedy gamblers on the Stock Exchange, idle officers of the army and navy (poor fellows!) worn-out mockers of the Clubs, desperate purveyors of exciting war-news for the comfortable breakfast tables of those who have nothing to lose by war." Such men were the enemies of the working class: they "cannot speak of your order, of its aims, of its leaders without a sneer or an insult." They "would deliver you bound hand and foot for ever to irresponsible capital." It was indeed a remarkable statement to come from a man who still regarded himself as a Liberal and who was, at the start, a warm admirer of Gladstone. In the course of the struggle Morris was to discover the hollowness both of Liberalism and of its great leader and was in the end no less disillusioned by the reformist Trade Union leaders, who, as he said later, he had found to be "quite under the influence of the Capitalist politicians."

THE RIVER OF FIRE

With this episode the negative part of Morris' political education was completed. He continued, and never underestimated the importance of, the craft work he was doing through the Firm and the fight to preserve Britain's architectural treasures through Anti-Scrape. He continued to write poetry because this was as natural and as necessary to him as breathing. But he saw more and more clearly that none of these things, still less activity within the framework of the established political system, were any solution for the evils of the world. A more fundamental remedy was needed, but what, and how, and by whom? His state of mind at this point is reflected in the first of his public lectures, and the first item in this volume, delivered at the end of 1877.

This lecture, which contains one of his most famous and characteristic aphorisms: "I do not want art for a few, any more than education for a few, or freedom for a few," shows that his criticism of society was already complete. He knows what he hates and knows what he wants, but when he has to come to a conclusion he is still vague as to the means. "I have a sort of faith . . . that men will get wiser as well as more learned . . . I believe that as we have now partly achieved LIBERTY, so we shall one day achieve EQUALITY, which, and which only, means FRATERNITY."

Yet his work with the Eastern Question Association had indeed given him the clue. He had seen the working class in action and he came to realise that here was the power which could change the world. With this realisation he passed from apathy and doubt to hope and confidence, the protester became a revolutionary. It is not easy today to realise just what a step this was at this date for a man in his position—rich, famous and busy—to pass from his own class and take the standpoint of the workers. It was indeed a new birth—"I was born once long ago: I am born again tonight," he makes the hero of *The Pilgrims of Hope* declare. And in a luminous passage, written as early as 1881, discussing the death of the old art, he had said:

"We of the English middle classes are the most powerful body of men that the world has yet seen . . . And yet when we come to look the matter in the face, we cannot fail to see that even for us with all our strength it will be a hard matter to bring about that birth of the new art: for between us and that which is to be, if art is not to perish utterly, there is something alive and devouring; something as it were a river of fire that will put all that tries to swim across to a hard proof indeed, and scare from the plunge every soul that is not made fearless by desire of truth and insight of the happy days to come beyond."[4]

This passage is certainly capable of a far wider application than is immediately apparent. Morris was indeed speaking of art, but already he refused to separate art from life, he understood that the new art can only spring from "the happy days" for which a social revolution will be needed. And by 1881 Morris was ready for the plunge into the river of fire which divides class from class.

By this time he had ceased to think of himself as a radical Liberal, and, as he explains to Andreas Scheu, "intended to join any body who distinctly called themselves Socialists." So, early in 1883, he joined the Democratic Federation (soon to be re-named the Social Democratic Federation) just founded by H. M. Hyndman. Of the failings of Hyndman it is unnecessary to speak here at any length. He was both sectarian and opportunist and he could never work with others as an equal. At the same time he had immense energy, and, if his understanding of Marxism was superficial and dogmatic, it was at least through him that Marxist ideas began to penetrate the British Labour Movement. Lenin characterised him, generously enough, as "a bourgeois philistine, who belonging to the best of his class, eventually struggles through to Socialism but never quite sheds his bourgeois conceptions and prejudices."[5]

If it was to him and to E. Belfort Bax that Morris owed his first introduction to Marxism, the disciple soon passed far beyond his masters, and it is Morris, rather than either

4 Thompson, op. cit., p. 282.
5 *Lenin in Britain*, p. 87.

Hyndman or Bax, who can properly be called the first English Marxist. This truth has been but slowly recognised, not only by the reformists and anarchists who each, in their own fashion, have tried to annex him, but also by Marxists. It was only with the work of R. Page Arnot and, later, Edward Thompson, that this has been generally recognised. Morris did not learn his Marxism by rote, but so absorbed it that in his propaganda writings he reshaped it into his own distinctive language—a language so different from that of most Socialist writers that its really quite orthodox content has often been overlooked.

Nevertheless to the attentive reader it is now clear enough that on the essential points Morris was neither utopian nor reformist but Marxist. This is all the more remarkable when we remember how little of the work of Marx and Engels was available to English readers in the eighty-eighties. Let us consider some of these essentials.

First, and by the early English Socialists it was always placed first, the question of exploitation. In his Socialist lectures Morris repeatedly explains that the capitalists, through their monopoly of the means of production, can force the workers to sell their labour power for less than its true value and that this is the source of their wealth. An example of this analysis may be found in *Useful Work versus Useless Toil*.[6] Morris always approached such questions in a historical rather than an abstract way. He saw this form of exploitation as the last of a series stretching back through the different kinds of class society, and that from it inevitably arises class struggle. This for him as for Marx is the clue to history and the only means by which Socialism can be won:

"It is most important that young Socialists should have this fact of the class-war always before them. It explains past history, and in the present gives us the only solid hope of the future. And it must be understood that it is only by

6 p. 86 of this volume.

the due working out of this class-war to its end, the *abolition of classes* that Socialism can come about . . . The middle-class semi-Socialists, driven by class instinct, preach
revolution without the class struggle: which is an absurdity
and an impossibility."

And:

"We can see that this class struggle cannot come to an end
till the classes themselves do: one class must absorb the
other. Which, then? Surely the useful one, the one the
world lives by, and on."[7]

And thirdly, again as a consequence of this clarity about
exploitation and class, he stood firmly by Marx's view of
the state as an organ of capitalist class rule which must be
destroyed:

"You must remember that all our law and government,
from Parliament to a County Court, has now got to be just
an elaborate defence of that very monopoly which it is our
business to clear away, though they by no means began
with that. True it is, that if the whole class of the workers
could be convinced on one day or in one year of the necessity of abolishing monopoly, it would pass away like the
clouds of night. But the necessities of the miserable and
the aspirations of the intelligent will outrun the slower
processes of conversion, and the anti-monopolists will find
themselves in a position in which they will be forced to try
to get hold of the executive, in order to destroy it and thus
metamorphose society, not in order to govern by it and as
they are now governed."[8]

IN THE MOVEMENT

From the moment of joining the Social Democratic Federation Morris changed his whole way of life, taking an active
part in every side of the work of the organisation. He

---

7 both quoted from Thompson, op. cit., p. 791.
8 from *Monopoly: or How Labour is Robbed*, Jackson, p. 206.

wrote, he lectured, he made himself, very much against his natural inclination, an effective outdoor speaker, he gave generous financial contributions. Professor E. D. Lemire in an appendix to *The Unpublished Lectures of William Morris* lists 578 meetings at which he is known to have spoken between 1883 and his death in 1896—there must have been a number of which we have no record. He was soon involved, too, in the disputes and antagonisms which arose within the Federation. Before long he found himself, very unwillingly, a leader of that section which was increasingly disgusted by the opportunism, dictatorial methods and love of intrigue of Hyndman and his supporters. This opposition was of a very mixed character. On the one hand were people like Eleanor Marx, Edward Aveling and Belfort Bax who wanted the Federation to develop into a real Socialist party with roots in the masses. On the other a number of anarchists who, whatever their personal merits, and Morris liked and respected a number of them, were hostile in principle to leadership and discipline.

By December 1884 an open break had developed. Morris and his supporters secured a 10 to 8 majority on the Executive against Hyndman and then surprised everyone by resigning *en bloc*. Morris saw that the rival factions would never be able to work amicably together, so, as he wrote to Mrs. Burne-Jones:

"Our lot agreed beforehand, being I must say moved by me, that it is not worth fighting for the name of the S.D.F. and the sad remains of *Justice* [the Federation's journal] at the expense of a month or two of wrangling: so as Hyndman considers the S.D.F. his property, let him take it and make what he can of it . . . and we will begin again quite clean-handed to try the more humdrum method of quiet propaganda, and start a new paper of our own."[9]

It is now possible to see that the split, though perhaps inevitable, was badly bungled. Morris was quite inex-

9 Henderson, op. cit., p. 222.

perienced at this kind of political in-fighting and though the case against Hyndman was formidable, the actual break came over a personal, and apparently trivial, difference and the underlying issues were never explained to the body of the membership. As Edward Thompson says:

"The fact was that to the rank and file the whole thing appeared as a mystery. They knew nothing of the history of the dispute, and the majority, by refusing to submit it to a general meeting, seemed afraid to consult them ... Morris and the majority allowed themselves to be provoked into taking action on the wrong issues and in the wrong way ... In the result, not only was Hyndman left in a position of strength, but the split was of necessity an ugly ragged split rather than a clean break."[10]

The members on the whole did not see why they should leave an organisation to which they had grown accustomed over an issue which they did not understand and which had never been explained to them.

The Socialist League, which the seceders proceeded to form, was therefore a minority body from the start and had to fish around for members where it could. More serious, perhaps, it could never quite make up its mind what it wanted to be or do. The Avelings and others, who came to be known as "the Parliamentarians" wanted to make it the core of a real Socialist Party, with roots in the Trade Unions and undertaking political activities in accordance with its strength and circumstances. On the other wing were a number of anarchists and near-anarchists wedded to a sterile leftism. And between the two Morris and those who shared his views, afraid of a repetition of Hyndman's adventurism, felt that, while not opposed in principle to practical political activities at some future date, the present task was, as the phrase went, "to make Socialists".

"Our view is that such a body [as the Socialist League] in

10 Thompson, op. cit., p. 420—1.

the present state of things has no function but to educate the people in the principles of Socialism, and to organize such as it can get hold of to take their due places, when the crisis shall come which will force action on us."

In the course of time these differences broke the League, and left Morris, who, though no anarchist, had sided with them against the Parliamentarians, as their prisoner. For some years he struggled to make the best of an impossible situation, until, as Shaw puts it:

"Morris, who had been holding the League up by the scruff of its neck, opened his hand, whereupon it dropped like a stone into the sea, leaving only a little wreckage to surface occasionally and demand bail at the police court or a small loan."[11]

Before this happened, however, the League had a number of years in which it did some remarkable work, and it can be said that the credit for its positive achievements belongs overwhelmingly to Morris himself. Making Socialists may have been too limited an objective but all his energies were devoted to it. He travelled constantly to every part of Britain and basic Socialist ideas were put for the first time, in a brilliant and attractive way, to thousands of workers. Lectures like *How We Live and How We Might Live* and *The Society of the Future* in this volume give an excellent idea of the quality of this propaganda.[12] The letters to his daughter Jane give a vivid picture of Morris at work in the movement,[13] while his account of Bloody Sunday—November 13th, 1887 illustrates his share in and his reactions to, one of the outstanding political happenings of the eighty-eighties.[14]

Bloody Sunday illustrates another concern of Morris—his desire for unity. Purist as he may have been in some

---

11 May Morris, *William Morris: Artist, Writer, Socialist*, vol. II, p. XVI.
12 pp. 134 and 188.
13 p. 182.
14 p. 205.

respects he was ready to co-operate with all who were carrying on a struggle against any aspect of capitalism and its state. Bloody Sunday was the climax of a campaign in which Socialists and Radicals of various complexions as well as Irish Nationalists had been protesting against coercion in Ireland and police methods at home. Two years earlier Morris had taken an active part in a prolonged free speech battle in London. In 1892, after the dissolution of the League he had initiated an attempt "to promote the alliance of Socialist organizations in Great Britain". A manifesto was issued over the signatures of Morris, of Hyndman (for the S.D.F.) and of Shaw (for the Fabian Society) but neither of these nor the organisations they represented were sufficiently in earnest over unity to make the plan a success and a real chance to set up a genuine Socialist Party was allowed to slip away. A year later another attempt, under very different auspices, was made with the foundation of the Independent Labour Party.

As a writer, too, Morris' contribution was outstanding, not only in books and pamphlets but as editor of the League's weekly journal, *Commonweal*. This he made the outstanding Socialist magazine of its time and to it he contributed some of his finest writings—not only *News from Nowhere* and *The Dream of John Ball*, but articles, reports, reviews and comments on current affairs. Some specimens of his *Commonweal* work are also included here.

After Morris left the Socialist League at the end of 1890 he continued to work in the Hammersmith Socialist Society, formed around the Hammersmith branch, which, under his direct leadership, had always been the largest and most active in the League. It has sometimes been suggested that his Socialist convictions had by then weakened. Some have even suggested that such a change dated from his experiences on Bloody Sunday. For this there ist no evidence at all, though it is true that he came to have a more realistic view of the size of the task confronting Socialists. If his activities decreased this was more than accounted for by the ill health of his last years, and they remained considerable by any ordinary standards almost to the end.

Indirectly, he perhaps answered the slander himself in his last outdoor speech, delivered on the occasion of the funeral of Sergius Stepniak. A previous speaker had suggested that in his later years Stepniak had lost some of his revolutionary fervour. Morris, for whom no time or place was unsuited for speaking the truth, responded with a characteristic impromptu: "This is a lie—to suggest that Stepniak had ceased to be a revolutionary. He died as he had lived, a revolutionary to the end."[15] And his very last lecture in the Hammersmith Clubroom on January 9th, 1896, had as its subject "One Socialist Party". On October 3rd he died.

MORRIS, MAN AND NATURE

In a short introduction such as this there must be many aspects of Morris' work and thinking left unnoticed, but one perhaps should be mentioned at a time when problems of man and his environment are beginning to attract more attention. Morris was deeply concerned for people, that they should lead free, happy and dignified lives in which all could develop to the full the powers with which, he was convinced, all are potentially endowed. But he knew that this was only possible given a healthy attidude to the natural world. He saw it, not, as capitalism has made it, an enemy to be conquered and exploited but as a friend to be won and cherished. His hatred of capitalism had perhaps been first aroused by the way it had gutted and defiled vast areas of the world—a process that in his time had scarcely begun. His passionate love of the earth as it had been shaped by thousands of years of co-operation

15 Thompson, op. cit., p. 722.

between man and his environment and his conviction that Socialism would renew that brutally interrupted co-operation comes out very strongly in *Under an Elm-Tree*,[16] included in this volume, but, indeed it is apparent in all his work. Thus he writes in *The Lesser Arts*:

"For there indeed if anywhere, in the English country when people cared about such things, was there a full sympathy between the works of man and the land they were made for. The land is a little land; too much shut up within the narrow seas, as it seems, to have much space for swelling into hugeness: there are no great wastes overwhelming in their dreariness, no great solitudes of forests, no terrible untrodden mountain walls: all is measured, mingled, varied, gliding easily one thing into another: little rivers, little plains, swelling, speedily changing uplands, all beset with handsome orderly trees; little hills, little mountains, netted over with the walls of sheep-walks: all is little; yet not foolish and blank, but serious rather, and abundant of meaning for such as choose to seek it: it is neither prison nor palace, but a decent home."

He believed that capitalism, which grows by creating imaginary wants, so that we are persuaded into buying ever increasing numbers of useless articles in order that profits may increase, has produced not happiness but increasing waste and pollution. Today, when experts are seriously beginning to calculate how long the earth's resources will last at the present rates of consumption, and how long it will be before all lakes and rivers are as poisoned and dead as Lake Erie, we can perhaps understand his concern better than ever before.

Morris forces upon us all the questions, How should a man live? How ought he to live? How do we want to live? And in answering them he directs our thoughts from quantity of possessions to the quality of our lives. We have been led, he suggests, to a false conception of civilisation:

16 p. 215.

"I had thought that civilization meant the attainment of peace and order and freedom, of goodwill between man and man, of the love of truth and the hatred of injustice, and by consequence the attainment of the good life which these things breed, a life free from craven fear, but full of incident: that is what I thought it meant, not more stuffed chairs and more cushions, and more carpets and gas, and more dainty meat and drink—and herewithal more and sharper differences between class and class."[17]

He distinguished sharply between wealth, by which he meant all that makes a nation healthy and prosperous, and riches, which are merely the counterpart of poverty:

"I tell you civilization will begin on the day when we determine that Riches and Poverty shall disappear into one commonweal of happy people."[18]

In *The Society of the Future*[19] he gives perhaps his fullest statement (apart from the fiction of *News from Nowhere*, for which it may be regarded as a preliminary sketch) of what a Socialist society might be like. It is a picture rightly tentative enough on details but uncompromising on some fundamental principles. It would be marked, he suggested, by a simplicity that would be far removed from asceticism but equally far from the luxury (for the few) which was characteristic of capitalism. That was a society of slaves and slave-owners—the life-style of free men must be something entirely different:

"When our opponents say, as they sometimes do, How should we be able to procure the luxuries of life in a Socialist society? answer boldly, We could not do so and we don't care, for we don't want them and won't have them; and indeed, I feel sure that we cannot if we are all free men together. Free men, I am sure, must lead simple lives and have simple pleasures: and if we shudder away

17 from *The Beauty of Life*, Cole, pp. 560—1.
18 May Morris, op. cit., p. 405.
19 p. 188.

from that necessity now, it is because we are not free men and have in consequence wrapped up our lives in such a complexity of dependence that we have grown feeble and helpless."

He never confused simplicity with poverty or drabness. In the review of Bellamy's *Looking Backward* which he wrote in 1889 for *Commonweal* he declared that variety of life was as much an aim of true Communism as equality of condition.

The working out of a truly self-renewing ecological basis for the earth may well be the next great task before humanity, a task impossible for capitalism, possible though still not easy for Socialism. The profound wisdom of William Morris can be of immense value to us in attempting it.

THE LESSER ARTS

[This was Morris' first lecture, given, under the title of "The Decorative Arts" to the Trades Guild of Learning, probably in the Co-operative Hall, Castle Street, Oxford Street, London, on April 12th, 1877. It was first published as a pamphlet in 1878 and subsequent reprintings include *Collected Works,* XXII, 3-27, Cole, 494-516 and Jackson, 17-37.

It is worth noting that even at this early date Morris gives the widest interpretation to art, as embracing all things made by men, and that he sees it as a social activity which must therefore be studied historically.]

HEREAFTER I hope in another lecture to have the pleasure of laying before you an historical survey of the lesser, or as they are called the Decorative Arts, and I must confess it would have been pleasanter to me to have begun my talk with you by entering at once upon the subject of the history of this great industry; but, as I have something to say in a third lecture about various matters connected with the practice of Decoration among ourselves in these days, I feel that I should be in a false position before you, and one that might lead to confusion, or over-much explanation, if I did not let you know what I think on the nature and scope of these arts, on their condition at the present time, and their outlook in times to come. In doing this it is like enough that I shall say things with which you will very much disagree; I must ask you there-fore from the outset to believe that whatever I may blame or whatever I may praise, I neither, when I think of what history has been, am inclined to lament the past, to despise the present, or despair of the future; that I believe all the change and stir about us is a sign of the world's life, and that it will lead—by ways, indeed, of which we have no guess—to the bettering of all mankind.

Now as to the scope and nature of these Arts I have to say, that though when I come more into the details of my subject I shall not meddle much with the great art of Architecture, and less still with the great arts commonly called Sculpture and Painting, yet I cannot in my own mind quite sever them from those lesser so-called Decorative Arts, which I have to speak about: it is only in latter times, and under the most intricate conditions of life, that they have fallen apart from one another; and I hold that, when they are so parted, it is ill for the Arts altogether: the lesser ones become trivial, mechanical, unintelligent, incapable of resisting the changes pressed upon them by fashion or dishonesty; while the greater, however they may be practised for a while by men of great minds and wonder-working hands, unhelped by the lesser, unhelped by each other, are sure to lose their dignity of popular arts, and become nothing but dull adjuncts to unmeaning pomp, or ingenious toys for a few rich and idle men.

However, I have not undertaken to talk to you of Architecture, Sculpture, and Painting, in the narrower sense of those words, since, most unhappily as I think, these master-arts, these arts more specially of the intellect, are at the present day divorced from decoration in its narrower sense. Our subject is that great body of art, by means of which men have at all times more or less striven to beautify the familiar matters of everyday life: a wide subject, a great industry; both a great part of the history of the world, and a most helpful instrument to the study of that history.

A very great industry indeed, comprising the crafts of house-building, painting, joinery and carpentry, smiths' work, pottery and glass-making, weaving, and many others: a body of art most important to the public in general, but still more so to us handicraftsmen; since there is scarce anything that they use, and that we fashion, but it has always been thought to be unfinished till it has had some touch or other of decoration about it. True it is that in many or most cases we have got so used to this ornament, that we look upon it as if it had grown of itself, and note it no more than the mosses on the dry sticks with which we light our fires. So much the worse! for there *is* the decoration, or some pretence of it, and it has, or ought to have, a use and a meaning. For, and this is at the root of the whole matter, everything made by man's hands has a form, which must be either beautiful or ugly; beautiful if it is in accord with Nature, and helps her; ugly if it is discordant with Nature, and thwarts her; it cannot be indifferent: we, for our parts, are busy or sluggish, eager or unhappy, and our eyes are apt to get dulled to this eventfulness of form in those things which we are always looking at. Now it is one of the chief uses of decoration, the chief part of its alliance with nature, that it has to sharpen our dulled senses in this matter: for this end are those wonders of intricate patterns interwoven, those strange forms invented, which men have so long delighted in: forms and intricacies that do not necessarily imitate nature, but in which the hand of the craftsman is guided to work in the way that she does, till the web, the cup, or the knife, look as natural, nay as lovely, as the green field, the river bank, or the mountain flint.

To give people pleasure in the things they must perforce *use,* that is one great office of decoration; to give people pleasure in the things they must perforce *make,* that is the other use of it.

Does not our subject look important enough now? I say that without these arts, our rest would be vacant and uninteresting, our labour mere endurance, mere wearing away of body and mind.

As for that last use of these arts, the giving us pleasure in our work, I scarcely know how to speak strongly enough of it; and yet if I did not know the value of repeating a truth again and again, I should have to excuse myself to you for saying any more about this, when I remember how a great man now living has spoken of it: I mean my friend

Professor John Ruskin: if you read the chapter in the 2nd vol. of his *Stones of Venice* entitled, "On the Nature of Gothic, and the Office of the Workman therein," you will read at once the truest and the most eloquent words that can possibly be said on the subject. What I have to say upon it can scarcely be more than an echo of his words, yet I repeat there is some use in reiterating a truth, lest it be forgotten; so I will say this much further: we all know what people have said about the curse of labour, and what heavy and grievous nonsense are the more part of their words thereupon; whereas indeed the real curses of craftsmen have been the curse of stupidity, and the curse of injustice from within and from without: no, I cannot suppose there is anybody here who would think it either a good life, or an amusing one, to sit with one's hands before one doing nothing—to live like a gentleman, as fools call it.

Nevertheless there *is* dull work to be done, and a weary business it is setting men about such work, and seeing them through it, and I would rather do the work twice over with my own hands than have such a job: but now only let the arts which we are talking of beautify our labour, and be widely spread, intelligent, well understood both by the maker and the user, let them grow in one word *popular*, and there will be pretty much an end of dull work and its wearing slavery; and no man will any longer have an excuse for talking about the curse of labour, no man will any longer have an excuse for evading the blessing of labour. I believe there is nothing that will aid the world's progress so much as the attainment of this; I protest there is nothing in the world that I desire so much as this, wrapped up, as I am sure it is, with changes political and social, that in one way or another we all desire.

Now if the objection be made, that these arts have been the handmaids of luxury, of tyranny and of superstition, I must needs say that it is true in a sense; they have been so used, as many other excellent things have been. But it is also true that, among some nations, their most vigorous and freest times have been the very blossoming times of art:

while at the same time, I must allow that these decorative arts have flourished among oppressed peoples, who have seemed to have no hope of freedom: yet I do not think that we shall be wrong in thinking that at such times, among such peoples, art, at least, was free; when it has not been, when it has really been gripped by superstition, or by luxury, it has straightway begun to sicken under that grip. Nor must you forget that when men say popes, kings, and emperors built such and such buildings, it is a mere way of speaking. You look in your history-books to see who built Westminster Abbey, who built St. Sophia at Constantinople, and they tell you Henry III, Justinian the Emperor. Did they? or, rather, men like you and me, handicraftsmen, who have left no names behind them, nothing but their work?

Now as these arts call people's attention and interest to the matters of every-day life in the present, so also, and that I think is no little matter, they call our attention at every step to that history, of which, I said before, they are so great a part; for no nation, no state of society, however rude, has been wholly without them: nay, there are peoples not a few, of whom we know scarce anything, save that they thought such and such forms beautiful. So strong is the bond between history and decoration, that in the practice of the latter we cannot, if we would, wholly shake off the influence of past times over what we do at present. I do not think it is too much to say that no man, however original he may be, can sit down to-day and draw the ornament of a cloth, or the form of an ordinary vessel or piece of furniture, that will be other than a development or a degradation of forms used hundreds of years ago; and these, too, very often, forms that once had a serious meaning, though they are now become little more than a habit of the hand; forms that were once perhaps the mysterious symbols of worships and beliefs now little remembered or wholly forgotten. Those who have diligently followed the delightful study of these arts are able as if through windows to look upon the life of the past:—the very first beginnings of thought among nations whom we cannot even name; the terrible empires of the ancient East; the free vigour and glory of Greece; the heavy weight, the firm grasp of Rome; the fall of her temporal Empire which spread so wide about the world all that good and evil which men can never forget, and never cease to feel; the clashing of East and West, South and North, about her rich and fruitful daughter Byzantium; the rise, the dissensions, and the waning of Islam; the wanderings of Scandinavia; the Crusades; the foundation of the States of modern Europe; the struggles of free thought with ancient dying system—with all these events and their meaning is the history of popular art interwoven; with all this, I say, the careful student of decoration as an historical industry must be familiar. When I think of this, and the usefulness of all this knowledge, at a time when history has become so earnest a study amongst us as to have given us, as it were, a new sense: at a time when we so long to know the reality of all that has happened, and are to be put off no longer with the dull records of the battles and intrigues of kings and scoundrels—I say when I think of all this, I hardly know how to say that this interweaving of the Decorative Arts with the history of the past is of less importance than their dealings with the life of the present: for should not these memories also be a part of our daily life?

And now let me recapitulate a little before I go further, before we begin to look into the condition of the arts at the present day. These arts, I have said, are part of a great system invented for the expression of a man's delight in beauty: all peoples and times have used them; they have been the joy of free nations, and the solace of oppressed nations; religion has used and elevated them, has abused and degraded them; they are connected with all history, and are clear teachers of it; and, best of all, they are the sweeteners of human labour, both to the handicraftsman, whose life is spent in working in them, and to people in general who are influenced by the sight of them at every turn of the day's work: they make our toil happy, our rest fruitful.

And now if all I have said seems to you but mere open-mouthed praise of these arts, I must say that it is not for nothing that what I have hitherto put before you has taken that form.

It is because I must now ask you this question: All these good things—will you have them? will you cast them from you?

Are you surprised at my question—you, most of whom, like myself, are engaged in the actual practice of the arts that are, or ought to be, popular?

In explanation, I must somewhat repeat what I have already said. Time was when the mystery and wonder of handicrafts were well acknowledged by the world, when imagination and fancy mingled with all things made by man, and in those days all handicraftsmen were *artists,* as we should now call them. But the thought of man became more intricate, more difficult to express; art grew a heavier thing to deal with, and its labour was more divided among great men, lesser men, and little men, till that art, which was once scarce more than a rest of body and soul, as the hand cast the shuttle or swung the hammer, became to some men so serious a labour, that their working lives have been one long tragedy of hope and fear, joy and trouble. This was the growth of art: like all growth, it was good and fruitful for awhile; like all fruitful growth, it grew into decay; like all decay of what was once fruitful, it will grow into something new.

Into decay; for as the arts sundered into the greater and the lesser, contempt on one side, carelessness on the other arose, both begotten of ignorance of that *philosophy* of the Decorative Arts, a hint of which I have tried just now to put before you. The artist came out from the handicraftsmen, and left them without hope of elevation, while he himself was left without the help of intelligent, industrious sympathy. Both have suffered; the artist no less than the workman. It is with art as it fares with a company of soldiers before a redoubt, when the captain runs forward full of hope and energy, but looks not behind him to see if his men are following, and they hang back, not knowing why they are brought there to die. The captain's life is spent for nothing, and his men are sullen prisoners in the redoubt of Unhappiness and Brutality.

I must in plain words say of the Decorative Arts, of all the arts, that it is not so much that we are inferior in them to all who have gone before us, but rather that they are in a state of anarchy and disorganization, which makes a sweeping change necessary and certain.

So that again I ask my question, All that good fruit which the arts should bear, will you have it? will you cast it from you? Shall that sweeping change that must come, be the change of loss or of gain?

We who believe in the continuous life of the world, surely we are bound to hope that the change will bring us gain and not loss, and to strive to bring that gain about.

Yet how the world may answer my question, who can say? A man in his short life can see but a little way ahead, and even in mine, wonderful and unexpected things have come to pass. I must needs say that therein lies my hope rather than in all I see going on round about us. Without disputing that if the imaginative arts perish, some new thing, at present unguessed of, *may* be put forward to supply their loss in men's lives, I cannot feel happy in that prospect, nor can I believe that mankind will endure such a loss for ever: but in the meantime the present state of the arts and their dealings with modern life and progress seem to me to point, in appearance at least, to this immediate future; that the world, which has for a long time busied itself about other matters than the arts, and has carelessly let them sink lower and lower, till many not uncultivated men, ignorant of what they once were, and hopeless of what they might yet be, look upon them with mere contempt; that the world, I say, thus busied and hurried, will one day wipe the slate, and be clean rid in her impatience of the whole matter with all this tangle and trouble.

And then—what then?

Even now amid the squalor of London it is hard to imagine what it will be. Architecture, Sculpture, Painting, with the crowd of lesser arts that belong to them, these, together with Music and Poetry, will be dead and forgotten, will no longer excite or amuse people in the least: for, once more, we must not deceive ourselves; the death of one art means the death of all; the only difference in their fate will be that the luckiest will be eaten the last—the luckiest, or the unluckiest: in all that has to do with beauty the invention and ingenuity of man will have come to a dead stop; and all the while Nature will go on with her eternal recurrence of lovely changes—spring, summer, autumn, and winter; sunshine, rain, and snow; storm and fair weather; dawn, noon, and sunset; day and night—ever bearing witness against man that he has deliberately chosen ugliness instead of beauty, and to live where he is strongest amidst squalor or blank emptiness.

You see, sirs, we cannot quite imagine it; any more, perhaps, than our forefathers of ancient London, living in the pretty, carefully whitened houses, with the famous church and its huge spire rising above them—than they, passing about the fair gardens running down to the broad river, could have imagined a whole county or more covered over with hideous hovels, big, middle-sized, and little, which should one day be called London.

Sirs, I say that this dead blank of the arts that I more than dread is difficult even now to imagine; yet I fear that I must say that if it does not come about, it will be owing to some turn of events which we cannot at present foresee: but I hold that if it does happen, it will only last for a time, that it will be but a burning up of the gathered weeds, so that the field may bear more abundantly. I hold that men would wake up after a while, and look round and find the dullness unbearable, and begin once more inventing, imitating, and imagining, as in earlier days.

That faith comforts me, and I can say calmly, if the blank space must happen, it must, and amidst its darkness the new seed must sprout. So it has been before: first comes birth, and hope scarcely conscious of itself; then the flower and fruit of mastery, with hope more than conscious enough, passing into insolence, as decay follows ripeness; and then—the new birth again.

Meantime it is the plain duty of all who look seriously on the arts to do their best to save the world from what at the best will be a loss, the result of ignorance and unwisdom; to prevent, in fact, that most discouraging of all changes, the supplying the place of an extinct brutality by a new one; nay, even if those who really care for the arts are so weak and few that they can do nothing else, it may be their business to keep alive some tradition, some memory of the past, so that the new life when it comes may not waste itself more than enough in fashioning wholly new forms for its new spirit.

To what side then shall those turn for help, who really understand the gain of a great art in the world, and the loss of peace and good life that must follow from the lack of it? I think that they must begin by acknowledging that the ancient art, the art of unconscious intelligence, as one should call it, which began without a date, at least so long ago as those strange and masterly scratchings on mammoth-bones and the like found but the other day in the drift—that this art of unconscious intelligence is all but dead; that what little of it is left lingers among half-civilized nations, and is growing coarser, feebler, less intelligent year by year; nay, it is mostly at the mercy of some commercial accident, such as the arrival of a few shiploads of European dye-stuffs or a few dozen orders from European merchants: this they must recognize, and must hope to see in time its place filled by a new art of conscious intelligence, the birth of wiser, simpler, freer ways of life than the world leads now, than the world has ever led.

I said, to *see* this in time; I do not mean to say that our own eyes will look upon it: it may be so far off, as indeed it seems to some, that many would scarcely think it worth while thinking of: but there are some of us who cannot turn our faces to the wall, or sit deedless because our hope seems somewhat dim; and, indeed, I think that while the signs of the last decay of the old art with all the evils that must follow in its train are only too obvious about us, so on the other hand there are not wanting signs of the new dawn beyond that possible night of the arts, of which I have before spoken; this sign chiefly, that there are some few at least, who are heartily discontented with things as they are, and crave for something better, or at least some promise of it—this best of signs: for I suppose that if some half-dozen men at any time earnestly set their hearts on something coming about which is not discordant with nature, it will come to pass one day or other; because it is not by accident that an idea comes into the heads of a few; rather they are pushed on, and forced to speak or act by something stirring in the heart of the world which would otherwise be left without expression.

By what means then shall those work who long for reform in the arts, and who shall they seek to kindle into eager desire for possession of beauty, and better still, for the development of the faculty that creates beauty?

People say to me often enough: If you want to make your art succeed and flourish, you must make it the fashion: a phrase which I confess annoys me; for they mean by it that I should spend one day over my work to two days in trying to convince rich, and supposed influential people, that they care very much for what they really do not care in the least, so that it may happen according to the proverb: *Bell-wether took the leap, and we all went over.* Well, such advisers are right if they are content

41

with the thing lasting but a little while; say till you can make a little money—if you don't get pinched by the door shutting too quickly: otherwise they are wrong: the people they are thinking of have too many strings to their bow, and can turn their backs too easily on a thing that fails, for it to be safe work trusting to their whims: it is not their fault, they cannot help it, but they have no chance of spending time enough over the arts to know anything practical of them, and they must of necessity be in the hands of those who spend their time in pushing fashion this way and that for their own advantage.

Sirs, there is no help to be got out of these latter, or those who let themselves be led by them: the only real help for the decorative arts must come from those who work in them; nor must they be led, they must lead.

You whose hands make those things that should be works of art, you must be all artists, and good artists too, before the public at large can take real interest in such things; and when you have become so, I promise you that you shall lead the fashion; fashion shall follow your hands obediently enough.

That is the only way in which we can get a supply of intelligent popular art: a few artists of the kind so called now, what can they do working in the teeth of difficulties thrown in their way by what is called Commerce, but which should be called greed of money? working help-lessly among the crowd of those who are ridiculously called manufacturers, i.e. handicraftsmen, though the more part of them never did a stroke of hand-work in their lives, and are nothing better than capitalists and salesmen. What can these grains of sand do, I say, amidst the enormous mass of work turned out every year which professes in some way to be decorative art, but the deco-ration of which no one heeds except the salesmen who have to do with it, and are hard put to it to supply the cravings of the public for something new, not for some-thing pretty?

The remedy, I repeat, is plain if it can be applied; the

handicraftsman, left behind by the artist when the arts sundered, must come up with him, must work side by side with him: apart from the difference between a great master and a scholar, apart from the differences of the natural bent of men's minds, which would make one man an imitative, and another an architectural or decorative artist, there should be no difference between those employed on strictly ornamental work; and the body of artists dealing with this should quicken with their art all makers of things into artists also, in proportion to the necessities and uses of the things they would make.

I know what stupendous difficulties, social and economical, there are in the way of this; yet I think that they seem to be greater than they are: and of one thing I am sure, that no real living decorative art is possible if this is impossible.

It is not impossible, on the contrary it is certain to come about, if you are at heart desirous to quicken the arts; if the world will, for the sake of beauty and decency, sacrifice some of the things it is so busy over (many of which I think are not very worthy of its trouble), art will begin to grow again; as for those difficulties above mentioned, some of them I know will in any case melt away before the steady change of the relative conditions of men; the rest, reason and resolute attention to the laws of nature, which are also the laws of art, will dispose of little by little: once more, the way will not be far to seek, if the will be with us.

Yet, granted the will, and though the way lies ready to us, we must not be discouraged if the journey seem barren enough at first, nay, not even if things seem to grow worse for a while: for it is natural enough that the very evil which has forced on the beginning of reform should look uglier, while on the one hand life and wisdom are building up the new, and on the other folly and deadness are hugging the old to them.

In this, as in all other matters, lapse of time will be needed before things seem to straighten, and the courage and patience that does not despise small things lying ready to be done; and care and watchfulness, lest we begin to build the wall ere the footings are well in; and always through all things much humility that is not easily cast down by failure, that seeks to be taught, and is ready to learn.

For your teachers, they must be Nature and History: as for the first, that you must learn of it is so obvious that I need not dwell upon that now: hereafter, when I have to speak more of matters of detail, I may have to speak of the manner in which you must learn of Nature. As to the second I do not think that any man but one of the highest genius could do anything in these days without much study of ancient art, and even he would be much hindered if he lacked it. If you think that this contradicts what I said about the death of that ancient art, and the necessity I implied for an art that should be characteristic of the present day, I can only say that, in these times of plenteous knowledge and meagre performance, if we do not study the ancient work directly and learn to understand it, we shall find ourselves influenced by the feeble work all round us, and shall be copying the better work through the copyists and *without* understanding it, which will by no means bring about intelligent art. Let us therefore study it wisely, be taught by it, kindled by it; all the while determining not to imitate or repeat it; to have either no art at all, or an art which we have made our own.

Yet I am almost brought to a stand-still when bidding you to study nature and the history of art, by remembering that this is London, and what it is like: how can I ask working men passing up and down these hideous streets day by day to care about beauty? If it were politics, we must care about that; or science, you could wrap yourselves up in the study of facts, no doubt, without much caring what goes on about you—but beauty! do you not see what terrible difficulties beset art, owing to a long neglect of art—and neglect of reason, too, in this

44

matter? It is such a heavy question by what effort, by what dead-lift, you can thrust this difficulty from you, that I must perforce set it aside for the present, and must at least hope that the study of history and its monuments will help you somewhat herein. If you can really fill your minds with memories of great works of art, and great times of art, you will, I think, be able to a certain extent to look through the aforesaid ugly surroundings, and will be moved to discontent of what is careless and brutal now, and will, I hope, at last be so much discontented with what is bad, that you will determine to bear no longer that shortsighted, reckless brutality of squalor that so disgraces our intricate civilization.

Well, at any rate, London is good for this, that it is well off for museums—which I heartily wish were to be got at seven days in the weeks instead of six, or at least on the only day on which an ordinarily busy man, one of the taxpayers who support them, can as a rule see them quietly—and certainly any of us who may have any natural turn for art must get more help from frequenting them than one can well say. It is true, however, that people need some preliminary instruction before they can get all the good possible to be got from the prodigious treasures of art possessed by the country in that form: there also one sees things in a piecemeal way: nor can I deny that there is something melancholy about a museum, such a tale of violence, destruction, and carelessness, as its treasured scraps tell us.

But moreover you may sometimes have an opportunity of studying ancient art in a narrow but a more intimate, a more kindly form, the monuments of our own land. Sometimes only, since we live in the middle of this world of brick and mortar, and there is little else left us amidst it, except the ghost of the great church at Westminster, ruined as its exterior is by the stupidity of the restoring architect, and insulted as its glorious interior is by the pompous undertakers' lies, by the vainglory and ignorance of the last two centuries and a half—little besides

that and the matchless Hall near it: but when we can get
beyond that smoky world, there, out in the country we
may still see the works of our fathers yet alive amidst
the very nature they were wrought into, and of which
they are so completely a part: for there indeed if anywhere, in the English country, in the days when people
cared about such things, was there a full sympathy between the works of man and the land they were made
for:—the land is a little land; too much shut up within the narrow seas, as it seems, to have much space for
swelling into hugeness: there are no great wastes overwhelming in their dreariness, no great solitudes of forests,
no terrible untrodden mountain-walls: all is measured,
mingled, varied, gliding easily one thing into another:
little rivers, little plains, swelling, speedily changing uplands, all beset with handsome orderly trees; little hills,
little mountains, netted over with the walls of sheep-
walks: all is little; yet not foolish and blank, but serious
rather, and abundant of meaning for such as choose to
seek it: it is neither prison nor palace, but a decent
home.

All which I neither praise nor blame, but say that so it
is: some people praise this homeliness overmuch, as
if the land were the very axle-tree of the world; so do not
I, nor any unblinded by pride in themselves and all that
belongs to them: others there are who scorn it and the
tameness of it: not I any the more: though it would indeed be hard if there were nothing else in the world, no
wonders, no terrors, no unspeakable beauties; yet when we
think what a small part of the world's history, past, present, and to come, is this land we live in, and how much
smaller still in the history of the arts, and yet how our
forefathers clung to it, and with what care and pains
they adorned it, this unromantic, uneventful-looking land
of England, surely by this too our hearts may be touched,
and our hope quickened.

For as was the land, such was the art of it while folk
yet troubled themselves about such things; it strove little

46

to impress people either by pomp or ingenuity: not unseldom it fell into commonplace, rarely it rose into majesty; yet was it never oppressive, never a slave's nightmare nor an insolent boast: and at its best it had an inventiveness, an individuality that grander styles have never overpassed: its best too, and that was in its very heart, was given as freely to the yeoman's house, and the humble village church, as to the lord's palace or the mighty cathedral: never coarse, though often rude enough, sweet, natural and unaffected, an art of peasants rather than of merchant-princes or courtiers, it must be a hard heart, I think, that does not love it: whether a man has been born among it like ourselves, or has come wonderingly on its simplicity from all the grandeur overseas. A peasant art, I say, and it clung fast to the life of the people, and still lived among the cottagers and yeomen in many parts of the country while the big houses were being built "French and fine": still lived also in many a quaint pattern of loom and printing-block, and embroiderer's needle, while overseas stupid pomp had extinguished all nature and freedom, and art was become, in France especially, the mere expression of that successful and exultant rascality, which in the flesh no long time afterwards went down into the pit for ever.

Such was the English art, whose history is in a sense at your doors, grown scarce indeed, and growing scarcer year by year, not only through greedy destruction, of which there is certainly less than there used to be, but also through the attacks of another foe, called nowadays "restoration."

I must not make a long story about this, but also I cannot quite pass it over, since I have pressed on you the study of these ancient monuments. Thus the matter stands: these old buildings have been altered and added to century after century, often beautifully, always historically; their very value, a great part of it, lay in that: they have suffered almost always from neglect also, often from violence (that latter a piece of history often far from uninteresting), but ordinary obvious mending would almost always have kept them standing, pieces of nature and of history.

But of late years a great uprising of ecclesiastical zeal, coinciding with a great increase of study, and consequently of knowledge of mediaeval architecture, has driven people into spending their money on these buildings, not merely with the purpose of repairing them, of keeping them safe, clean, and wind-and water-tight, but also of "restoring" them to some ideal state of perfection; sweeping away if possible all signs of what has befallen them at least since the Reformation, and often since dates much earlier: this has sometimes been done with much disregard of art and entirely from ecclesiastical zeal, but oftener it has been well meant enough as regards art: yet you will not have listened to what I have said to-night if you do not see that from my point of view this restoration must be as impossible to bring about, as the attempt at it is destructive to the buildings so dealt with: I scarcely like to think what a great part of them have been made nearly useless to students of art and history: unless you knew a great deal about architecture you perhaps would scarce understand what terrible damage has been done by that dangerous "little knowledge" in this matter: but at least it is easy to be understood, that to deal recklessly with valuable (and national) monuments which, when once gone, can never be replaced by any splendour of modern art, is doing a very sorry service to the State.

You will see by all that I have said on this study of ancient art that I mean by education herein something much wider than the teaching of a definite art in schools of design, and that it must be something that we must do more or less for ourselves: I mean by it a systematic concentration of our thoughts on the matter, a studying of it in all ways, careful and laborious practice of it, and a determination to do nothing but what is known to be good in workmanship and design.

Of course, however, both as an instrument of that study we have been speaking of, as well as of the practice of the arts, all handicraftsmen should be taught to draw very carefully; as indeed all people should be taught drawing who are not physically incapable of learning it: but the art of drawing so taught would not be the art of designing, but only a means towards *this* end, *general capability in dealing with the arts.*

For I wish specially to impress this upon you, that *designing* cannot be taught at all in a school: continued practice will help a man who is naturally a designer, continual notice of nature and of art: no doubt those who have some faculty for designing are still numerous, and they want from a school certain technical teaching, just as they want tools: in these days also, when the best school, the school of successful practice going on around you, is at such a low ebb, they do undoubtedly want instruction in the history of the arts: these two things schools of design can give: but the royal road of a set of rules deduced from a sham science of design, that is itself not a science but another set of rules, will lead nowhere—or, let us rather say, to beginning again.

As to the kind of drawing that should be taught to men engaged in ornamental work, there is only *one best* way of teaching drawing, and that is teaching the scholar to draw the human figure: both because the lines of a man's body are much more subtle than anything else, and because you can more surely be found out and set right if you go wrong. I do think that such teaching as this, given to all people who care for it, would help the revival of the arts very much: the habit of discriminating between right and wrong, the sense of pleasure in drawing a good line, would really, I think, be education in the due sense of the word for all such people as had the germs of invention in them; yet as aforesaid, in this age of the world it would be mere affectation to pretend to shut one's eyes to the art of past ages: that also we must study. If other circumstances, social and economical, do not stand in our way, that is to say, if the world is not too busy to allow us to have Decorative Arts at all, these two are the *direct* means by which we shall get them; that is, general culti-vation of the powers of the mind, general cultivation of the powers of the eye and hand.

Perhaps that seems to you very commonplace advice and a very roundabout road; nevertheless 'tis a certain one, if by any road you desire to come to the new art, which is my subject to-night: if you do not, and if those germs of invention, which, as I said just now, are no doubt still common enough among men, are left neglected and undeveloped, the laws of Nature will assert them-selves in this as in other matters, and the faculty of design itself will gradually fade from the race of man. Sirs, shall we approach nearer to perfection by casting away so large a part of that intelligence which makes us *men?*

And now before I make an end, I want to call your attention to certain things, that, owing to our neglect of the arts for other business, bar that good road to us and are such an hindrance, that, till they are dealt with, it is hard even to make a beginning of our endeavour. And if my talk should seem to grow too serious for our subject, as indeed I think it cannot do, I beg you to remember what I said earlier, of how the arts all hang together. Now there is one art of which the old architect of Edward the Third's time was thinking—he who founded New Col-lege at Oxford, I mean — when he took this for his motto: "Manners maketh man": he meant by manners the art of morals, the art of living worthily, and like a man. I must needs claim this art also as dealing with my subject.

There is a great deal of sham work in the world, hurt-ful to the buyer, more hurtful to the seller, if he only knew it, most hurtful to the maker: how good a foundation it would be towards getting good Decorative Art, that is ornamental workmanship, if we craftsmen were to resolve to turn out nothing but excellent workmanship in all things, instead of having, as we too often have now, a very low average standard of work, which we often fall below.

I do not blame either one class or another in this mat-ter, I blame all: to set aside our own class of handicraftsmen, of whose shortcomings you and I know so much that we need talk no more about it, I know that the public in general are set on having things cheap, being so ignorant that they do not know when they get them nasty also; so ignorant that they neither know nor care whether they give a man his due: I know that the manufacturers (so called) are so set on carrying out competition to its utmost, competition of cheapness, not of excellence, that they meet the bargain-hunters half way, and cheerfully furnish them with nasty wares at the cheap rate they are asked for, by means of what can be called by no prettier name than fraud. England has of late been too much busied with the counting-house and not enough with the workshop: with the result that the counting-house at the present moment is rather barren of orders.

I say all classes are to blame in this matter, but also I say that the remedy lies with the handicraftsmen, who are not ignorant of these things like the public, and who have no call to be greedy and isolated like the manufacturers or middlemen; the duty and honour of educating the public lies with them, and they have in them the seeds of order and organization which make that duty the easier.

When will they see to this and help to make men of us all by insisting on this most weighty piece of manners; so that we may adorn life with the pleasure of cheerfully *buying* goods at their due price; with the pleasure of *selling* goods that we could be proud of both for fair price and fair workmanship: with the pleasure of working soundly and without haste at *making* goods that we could be proud of?—much the greatest pleasure of the three is that last, such a pleasure as, I think, the world has none like it.

You must not say that this piece of manners lies out of my subject: it is essentially a part of it and most important: for I am bidding you learn to be artists, if art is not to come to an end amongst us: and what is an artist but a workman who is determined that, whatever else happens, his work shall be excellent? or, to put it in another way: the decoration of workmanship, what is it but the expression of man's pleasure in successful labour? But what pleasure can there be in *bad* work, in *un*successful labour; why should we decorate *that*? and how can we bear to be always unsuccessful in our labour?

As greed of unfair gain, wanting to be paid for what we have not earned, cumbers our path with this tangle of bad work, of sham work, so that heaped-up money which this greed has brought us (for greed will have its way, like all other strong passions), this money, I say, gathered into heaps little and big, with all the false distinction which so unhappily it yet commands amongst us, has raised up against the arts a barrier of the love of luxury and show, which is of all obvious hindrances the worst to overpass: the highest and most cultivated classes are not free from the vulgarity of it, the lower are not free from its pretence. I beg you to remember both as a remedy against this, and as explaining exactly what I mean, that nothing can be a work of art which is not useful; that is to say, which does not minister to the body when well under command of the mind, or which does not amuse, soothe, or elevate the mind in a healthy state. What tons upon tons of unutterable rubbish pretending to be works of art in some degree would this maxim clear out of our London houses, if it were understood and acted upon! To my mind it is only here and there (out of the kitchen) that you can find in a well-to-do house things that are of any use at all: as a rule all the decoration (so called) that has got there is there for the sake of show, not because anybody likes it. I repeat, this stupidity goes through all classes of society: the silk curtains in my Lord's drawing-room are no more a matter of art to him than the powder in his footman's hair; the kitchen in a country farmhouse is most commonly a pleasant and homelike place, the parlour dreary and useless.

Simplicity of life, begetting simplicity of taste, that is, a love for sweet and lofty things, is of all matters most necessary for the birth of the new and better art we crave for; simplicity everywhere, in the palace as well as in the cottage.

Still more is this necessary, cleanliness and decency

everywhere, in the cottage as well as in the palace: the lack of that is a serious piece of *manners* for us to correct: that lack and all the inequalities of life, and the heaped-up thoughtlessness and disorder of so many centuries that cause it: and as yet it is only a very few men who have begun to think about a remedy for it in its widest range: even in its narrower aspect, in the defacements of our big towns by all that commerce brings with it, who heeds it? who tries to control their squalor and hideousness? there is nothing but thoughtlessness and recklessness in the matter; the helplessness of people who don't live long enough to do a thing themselves, and have not manliness and foresight enough to begin the work, and pass it on to those that shall come after them.

Is money to be gathered? cut down the pleasant trees among the houses, pull down ancient and venerable buildings for the money that a few square yards of London dirt will fetch; blacken rivers, hide the sun and poison the air with smoke and worse, and it's nobody's business to see to it or mend it: that is all that modern commerce, the counting-house forgetful of the workshop, will do for us herein.

And Science—we have loved her well, and followed her diligently, what will she do? I fear she is so much in the pay of the counting-house, the counting-house and the drill-sergeant, that she is too busy, and will for the present do nothing. Yet there are matters which I should have thought easy for her; say for example teaching Manchester how to consume its own smoke, or Leeds how to get rid of its superfluous black dye without turning it into the river, which would be as much worth her attention as the production of the heaviest of heavy black silks, or the biggest of useless guns. Anyhow, however it be done, unless people care about carrying on their business without making the world hideous, how can they care abourt Art? I know it will cost much both of time and money to better these things even a little; but I do not see how these can be better spent than in making life cheerful and honourable for others and for ourselves; and the gain of good life to the country at large that would result from men seriously setting about the bettering of the decency of our big towns would be priceless, even if nothing specially good befell the arts in consequence: I do not know that it would; but I should begin to think matters hopeful if men turned their attention to such things, and I repeat that, unless they do so, we can scarcely even begin, with any hope, our endeavours for the bettering of the arts.

Unless something or other is done to give all men some pleasure for the eyes and rest for the mind in the aspect of their own and their neighbours' houses, until the contrast is less disgraceful between the fields where beasts live and the streets where men live, I suppose that the practice of the arts must be mainly kept in the hands of a few highly cultivated men, who can go often to beautiful places, whose education enables them, in the contemplation of the past glories of the world, to shut out from their view the every-day squalors that the most of men move in.

Sirs, I believe that art has such sympathy with cheerful freedom, open-heartedness and reality, so much she sickens under selfishness and luxury, that she will not live thus isolated and exclusive, I will go further than this and say that on such terms I do not wish her to live. I protest that it would be a shame to an honest artist to enjoy what he had huddled up to himself of such art, as it would be for a rich man to sit and eat dainty food amongst starving soldiers in a beleaguered fort.

I do not want art for a few, any more than education for a few, or freedom for a few.

No, rather than art should live this poor thin life among a few exceptional men, despising those beneath them for an ignorance for which they themselves are responsible, for a brutality that they will not struggle with—rather than this, I would that the world should indeed sweep away all art for awhile, as I said before I thought it possible she might do; rather than the wheat should rot in the miser's granary, I would that the earth had it, that it might yet have a chance to quicken in the dark.

I have a sort of faith, though, that this clearing away of all art will not happen, that men will get wiser, as well as more learned; that many of the intricacies of life, on which we now pride ourselves more than enough, partly because they are new, partly because they have come with the gain of better things, will be cast aside as having played their part, and being useful no longer. I hope that we shall have leisure from war—war commercial, as well as war of the bullet and the bayonet; leisure from the knowledge that darkens counsel; leisure above all from the greed of money, and the craving for that overwhelming distinction that money now brings: I believe that as we have even now partly achieved Liberty, so we shall one day achieve Equality, which, and which only, means Fraternity, and so have leisure from poverty and all its griping, sordid cares.

Then having leisure from all these things, amidst renewed simplicity of life we shall have leisure to think about our work, that faithful daily companion, which no man any longer will venture to call the Curse of labour: for surely then we shall be happy in it, each in his place, no man grudging at another; no one bidden to be any man's *servant*, every one scorning to be any man's *master*: men will then assuredly be happy in their work, and that happiness will assuredly bring forth decorative, noble, *popular* art.

That art will make our streets as beautiful as the woods, as elevating as the mountain-sides: it will be a pleasure and a rest, and not a weight upon the spirits to come from the open country into a town; every man's house will be fair and decent, soothing to his mind and helpful to his work: all the works of man that we live amongst and handle will be in harmony with nature, will be reasonable and beautiful: yet all will be simple and inspiriting, not childish nor enervating; for as nothing of beauty and splendour that man's mind and hand may compass shall be wanting from our public buildings, so in no private dwelling will there be any signs of waste, pomp or insolence, and every man will have his share of the *best*.

It is a dream, you may say, of what has never been and never will be; true, it has never been, and therefore, since the world is alive and moving yet, my hope is the greater that it one day will be: true it is a dream; but dreams have before now come about of things so good and necessary to us, that we scarcely think of them more than of the daylight, though once people had to live without them, without even the hope of them.

Anyhow, dreams as it is, I pray you to pardon my setting it before you, for it lies at the bottom of all my work in the Decorative Arts, nor will it ever be out of my thoughts: and I am here with you to-night to ask you to help me in realizing this dream, this *hope*.

[One of Morris' earliest Socialist lectures, delivered in the
hall of University College, Oxford, on November 14th,
1883. John Ruskin was in the chair. First published in *To-
Day*, February and March, 1884. *Collected Works*, XXIII,
164—91, Jackson, 132—55.

This lecture caused a considerable uproar: its offence
was not so much over its Socialist ideas as because Morris
declared himself a member of an organisation and asked
his hearers to support it. *The Times* commented: "Mr. Morris announced himself a member of a socialistic society and
appealed for funds for the objects of the society. The Master of University then said to the effect that if he had
announced this beforehand it was probable that the Col-
lege-hall would have been refused."]

YOU may well think I am not here to criticize any special
school of art or artist, or to plead for any special style, or
to give you any instructions, however general, as to the
practice of the arts. Rather I want to take counsel with you
as to what hindrances may lie in the way towards making
art what it should be, a help and solace to the daily life of
all men. Some of you here may think that the hindrances in
the way are none, or few, and easy to be swept aside. You
will say that there is on many sides much knowledge of the
history of art, and plenty of taste for it, at least among the
cultivated classes; that many men of talent, and some few
of genius, practise it with no mean success; that within the
last fifty years there has been something almost like a fresh
renaissance of art, even in directions where such a change
was least to be hoped for. All this is true as far as it goes;
and I can well understand this state of things being a cause

of gratulation amongst those who do not know what the scope of art really is, and how closely it is bound up with the general condition of society, and especially with the lives of those who live by manual labour and whom we call the working classes. For my part, I cannot help noting that under the apparent satisfaction with the progress of art of late years there lies in the minds of most thinking people a feeling of mere despair as to the prospects of art in the future; a despair which seems to me fully justified if we look at the present condition of art without considering the causes which have led to it, or the hopes which may exist for a change in those causes. For, without beating about the bush, let us consider what the real state of art is. And first I must ask you to extend the word art beyond those matters which are consciously works of art, to take in not only painting and sculpture, and architecture, but the shapes and colours of all household goods, nay, even the arrangement of the fields for tillage and pasture, the management of towns and of our highways of all kinds; in a word, to extend it to the aspect of all the externals of our life. For I must ask you to believe that every one of the things that goes to make up the surroundings among which we live must be either beautiful or ugly, either elevating or degrading to us, either a torment and burden to the maker of it to make, or a pleasure and a solace to him. How does it fare therefore with our external surroundings in these days? What kind of an account shall we be able to give to those who come after us of our dealings with the earth, which our forefathers handed down to us still beautiful, in spite of all the thousands of years of strife and carelessness and selfishness?

Surely this is no light question to ask ourselves; nor am I afraid that you will think it a mere rhetorical flourish if I say that it is a question that may well seem a solemn one when it is asked here in Oxford, amidst sights and memories which we older men at least regard with nothing short of love. He must be indeed a man of narrow incomplete mind, who, amidst the buildings raised by the hopes of our forefathers, amidst the country which they made so lovely, would venture to say that the beauty of the earth was a matter of little moment. And yet, I say, how have we of these latter days treated the beauty of the earth, or that which we call art?

Perhaps I had best begin by stating what will scarcely be new to you, that art must be broadly divided into two kinds, of which we may call the first Intellectual, and the second Decorative Art, using the words as mere forms of convenience. The first kind addresses itself wholly to our mental needs; the things made by it serve no other purpose but to feed the mind, and, as far as material needs go, might be done without altogether. The second, though so much of it as is art does also appeal to the mind, is always but a part of things which are intended primarily for the service of the body. I must further say that there have been nations and periods which lacked the purely Intellectual art but positively none which lacked the Decorative (or at least some pretence of it); and furthermore, that in all times when the arts were in a healthy condition there was an intimate connexion between the two kinds of art; a connexion so close, that in the times when art flourished most, the higher and lower kinds were divided by no hard and fast lines. The highest intellectual art was meant to please the eye, as the phrase goes, as well as to excite the emotions and train the intellect. It appealed to all men, and to all the faculties of a man. On the other hand, the humblest of the ornamental art shared in the meaning and emotion of the intellectual; one melted into the other by scarce perceptible gradations; in short, the best artist was a workman still, the humblest workman was an artist. This is not the case now, nor has been for two or three centuries in civilized countries. Intellectual art is separated from Decorative by the sharpest lines of demarcation, not only as to the kind of work produced under those names, but even in the social position of the producers; those who follow the Intellectual arts being all professional men or gentlemen by virtue of their calling, while those who follow the Decorative are workmen earning weekly wages, non-gentlemen in short.

Now, as I have already said, many men of talent and some few of genius are engaged at present in producing works of Intellectual art, paintings and sculpture chiefly. It is nowise my business here or elsewhere to criticize their works; but my subject compels me to say that those who follow the Intellectual arts must be divided into two sections, the first composed of men who would in any age of the world have held a high place in their craft; the second of men who hold their position of gentleman-artist either by the accident of their birth, or by their possessing industry, business habits, or such-like qualities, out of all proportion to their artistic gifts. The work which these latter produce seems to me of little value to the world, though there is a thriving market for it, and their position is neither dignified nor wholesome; yet they are mostly not to be blamed for it personally, since often they have gifts for art, though not great ones, and would probably not have succeeded in any other career. They are, in fact, good decorative workmen spoiled by a system which compels them to ambitious individualist effort, by cutting off from them any opportunity for co-operation with others of greater or less capacity for the production of popular art.

As to the first section of artists, who worthily fill their places and make the world wealthier by their work, it must be said of them that they are very few. These men have won their mastery over their craft by dint of incredible toil, pains, and anxiety, by qualities of mind and strength of will which are bound to produce something of value. Nevertheless they are injured also by the system which insists on individualism and forbids co-operation. For first, they are cut off from tradition, that wonderful, almost miraculous accumulation of the skill of ages, which men find themselves partakers in without effort on their part. The knowledge of the past and the sympathy with it which the artists of to-day have, they have acquired, on the contrary, by their own most strenuous individual effort; and as that tradition no longer exists to help them in their practice of the art, and they are heavily weighted in the race by having to learn everything from the beginning, each man for himself, so also, and that is worse, the lack of it deprives them of a sympathetic and appreciative audience.

Apart from the artists themselves and a few persons who would be also artists but for want of opportunity and for insufficient gifts of hand and eye, there is in the public of to-day no real knowledge of art, and little love for it. Nothing, save at the best certain vague prepossessions, which are but the phantom of that tradition which once bound artist and public together. Therefore the artists are obliged to express themselves, as it were, in a language not understanded of the people. Nor is this their fault. If they were to try, as some think they should, to meet the public half-way and work in such a manner as to satisfy at any cost those vague prepossessions of men ignorant of art, they would be casting aside their special gifts, they would be traitors to the cause of art, which it is their duty and glory to serve. They have no choice save to do their own personal individual work unhelped by the present, stimulated by the past, but shamed by it, and even in a way hampered by it; they must stand apart as possessors of some sacred mystery which, whatever happens, they must at least do their best to guard. It is not to be doubted that both their own lives and their works are injured by this isolation. But the loss of the people; how are we to measure that? That they should have great men living and working amongst them, and be ignorant of the very existence of their work, and incapable of knowing what it means if they could see it!

In the times when art was abundant and healthy, all men were more or less artists; that is to say, the instinct for beauty which is inborn in every complete man had such force that the whole body of craftsmen habitually and without conscious effort made beautiful things, and the audience for the authors of intellectual art was nothing short of the whole people. And so they had each an assured hope of gaining that genuine praise and sympathy which all men who exercise their imagination in expression most certainly and naturally crave, and the lack of which does certainly injure them in some way; makes them shy, over-sensitive, and narrow, or else cynical and mocking, and in that case well-nigh useless. But in these days, I have said and repeat, the whole people is careless and ignorant of art; the inborn instinct for beauty is checked and thwarted at every turn; and the result on the less intellectual or decorative art is that as a spontaneous and popular expression of the instinct for beauty it does not exist at all.

It is a matter of course that everything made by man's hand is now obviously ugly, unless it is made beautiful by conscious effort; nor does it mend the matter that men have not lost the habit deduced from the times of art, of professing to ornament household goods and the like; for this sham ornament, which has no least intention of giving any-one pleasure, is so base and foolish that the words uphol-stery and upholsterer have come to have a kind of second-ary meaning indicative of the profound contempt which all sensible men have for such twaddle.

This, so far, is what decorative art has come to, and I must break off a while here and ask you to consider what it once was, lest you think over hastily that its degradation is a matter of little moment. Think, I beg you, to go no further back in history, of the stately and careful beauty of S. Sophia at Constantinople, of the golden twilight of S. Mark's at Venice; of the sculptured cliffs of the great French cathedrals, of the quaint and familiar beauty of our own minsters; nay, go through Oxford streets and ponder on what is left us there unscathed by the fury of the thriv-ing shop and the progressive college; or wander some day through some of the out-of-the-way villages and little towns that lie scattered about the country-side within twenty miles of Oxford; and you will surely see that the loss of decora-tive art is a grievous loss to the world.

Thus then in considering the state of art among us I have been driven to the conclusion that in its co-operative form it is extinct, and only exists in the conscious efforts of men of genius and talent, who themselves are injured, and thwarted, and deprived of due sympathy by the lack of co-operative art.

But furthermore, the repression of the instinct for beauty which has destroyed the Decorative and injured the Intellectual arts has not stopped there in the injury it has done us. I can myself sympathize with a feeling which I suppose is still not rare, a craving to escape sometimes to mere Nature, not only from ugliness and squalor, not only from a condition of superabundance of art, but even from a condition of art severe and well ordered, even, say, from such surroundings as the lovely simplicity of Periclean Athens. I can deeply sympathize with a weary man finding his account in interest in mere life and communion with external nature, the face of the country, the wind and weather, and the course of the day, and the lives of animals, wild and domestic; and man's daily dealings with all this for his daily bread, and rest, and innocent beast-like pleasure. But the interest in the mere animal life of man has become impossible to be indulged in in its fulness by most civilized people. Yet civilization, it seems to me, owes us some compensation for the loss of this romance, which now only hangs like a dream about the country life of busy lands. To keep the air pure and the rivers clean, to take some pains to keep the meadows and tillage as pleasant as reasonable use will allow them to be; to allow peaceable citizens freedom to wander where they will, so they do no hurt to garden or cornfield; nay, even to leave here and there some piece of waste or mountain sacredly free from fence or tillage as a memory of man's ruder struggles with nature in his earlier days: is it too much to ask civilization to be so far thoughtful of man's pleasure and rest, and to help so far as this her children to whom she has most often set such heavy tasks of grinding labour? Surely not an unreasonable asking. But not a whit of it shall we get under the present system of society. That loss of the instinct for beauty which has involved us in the loss of popular art is also busy in depriving us of the only compensation possible for that loss, by surely and not slowly destroying the beauty of the very face of the earth. Not only are London and our other great commercial cities mere masses of sordidness, filth, and squalor, embroidered with patches of pompous and vulgar hideousness, no less revolting to the eye and the mind when one knows what it means: not only have whole counties of England, and the heavens that hang over them, disappeared beneath a crust of unutterable grime, but the disease, which, to a visitor coming from the times of art, reason, and order, would seem to be a love of dirt and ugliness for its own sake, spreads all over the country, and every little market-town seizes the opportunity to imitate, as far as it can, the majesty of the hell of London and Manchester. Need I speak to you of the wretched suburbs that sprawl all round our fairest and most ancient cities? Must I speak to you of the degradation that has so speedily befallen this city, still the most beautiful of them all; a city which, with its surroundings, would, if we had had a grain of common sense, have been treated like a most precious jewel, whose beauty was to be preserved at any cost? I say at any cost, for it was a possession which did not belong to us, but which we were trustees of for all posterity. I am old enough to know how we have treated that jewel; as if it were any common stone kicking about on the highway, good enough to throw at a dog. When I remember the contrast between the Oxford of to-day and the Oxford which I first saw thirty years ago, I wonder I can face the misery (there is no other word for it) of visiting it, even to have the honour of addressing you to-night. But furthermore, not only are the cities a disgrace to us, and the smaller towns a laughing-stock; not only are the dwellings of man grown inexpressibly base and ugly, but the very cowsheds and cart-stables, nay, the merest piece of necessary farm-engineering, are tarred with the same brush. Even if a tree is cut down or blown down, a worse one, if any, is planted in its stead, and, in short, our civilization is passing like a blight, daily growing heavier and more poisonous, over the whole face of the country, so that every change is sure to be a change for the worse in its outward aspect. So then it comes to this, that not only are the minds of great artists narrowed and their sympathies frozen by their isolation, not only has co-operative art come to a standstill, but the very food on which both the greater and the lesser art subsists is being destroyed; the well of art is poisoned at its spring.

Now I do not wonder that those who think that these evils are from henceforth for ever necessary to the progress of civilization should try to make the best of things, should shut their eyes to all they can, and praise the galvanized life of the art of the present day; but, for my part, I believe that they are not necessary to civilization, but only accompaniments to one phase of it, which will change and pass into something else, like all prior phases have done. I believe also that the essential characteristic of the present state of society is that which has so ruined art, or the pleasure of life; and that this having died out, the inborn love of man for beauty and the desire for expressing it will no longer be repressed, and art will be free. At the same time I not only admit, but declare, and think it most important to declare, that so long as the system of competition in the production and exchange of the means of life goes on, the degradation of the arts will go on; and if that system is to last for ever, then art is doomed, and will surely die; that is to say, civilization will die. I know it is at present the received opinion that the competitive or "Devil take the hindmost" system is the last system of economy which the world will see; that it is perfection, and therefore finality has been reached in it; and it is doubtless a bold thing to fly in the face of this opinion, which I am told is held even by the most learned men. But though I am not learned, I have been taught that the patriarchal system died out into that of the citizen and chattel slave, which in its turn gave place to that of the feudal lord and the serf, which, passing through a modified form, in which the burgher, the gild-craftsman and his journeyman played their parts, was supplanted by the system of so-called free contract now existing. That all things since the beginning of the world have been tending to the development of this system I willingly admit, since it exists; that all the events of history have taken place for the purpose of making it eternal, the very evolution of those events forbids me to believe.

For I am "one of the people called Socialists"; therefore I am certain that evolution in the economical conditions of life will go on, whatever shadowy barriers may be drawn across its path by men whose apparent self-interest binds them, consciously or unconsciously, to the present, and who are therefore hopeless for the future. I hold that the condition of competition between man and man is bestial only, and that of association human; I think that the change from the undeveloped competition of the Middle Ages, trammelled as it was by the personal relations of feudality, and the attempts at associations of the gild-craftsmen into the full-blown *laissez-faire* competition of the nineteenth century, is bringing to birth out of its own anarchy, and by the very means by which it seeks to perpetuate that anarchy, a spirit of association founded on that antagonism which has produced all former changes in the condition of men, and which will one day abolish all classes and take definite and practical form, and substitute association for competition in all that relates to the production and exchange of the means of life. I further believe that as that change will be beneficent in many ways, so especially will it give an opportunity for the new birth of art, which is now being crushed to death by the money-bags of competitive commerce.

My reason for this hope for art is founded on what I feel quite sure is a truth, and an important one, namely that all art, even the highest, is influenced by the conditions of labour of the mass of mankind, and that any pretensions which may be made for even the highest intellectual art to be independent of these general conditions are futile and vain; that is to say, that any art which professes to be founded on the special education or refinement of a limited body or class must of necessity be unreal and

66

short-lived. Art is man's expression of his joy in labour. If those are not Professor Ruskin's words they embody at least his teaching on this subject. Nor has any truth more important ever been stated; for if pleasure in labour be generally possible, what a strange folly it must be for men to consent to labour without pleasure; and what a hideous injustice it must be for society to compel most men to labour without pleasure! For since all men not dishonest must labour, it becomes a question either of forcing them to lead unhappy lives or allowing them to live unhappily. Now the chief accusation I have to bring against the modern state of society is that it is founded on the art-lacking or unhappy labour of the greater part of men; and all that external degradation of the face of the country of which I have spoken is hateful to me not only because it is a cause of unhappiness to some few of us who still love art, but also and chiefly because it is a token of the unhappy life forced on the great mass of the population by the system of competitive commerce.

The pleasure which ought to go with the making of every piece of handicraft has for its basis the keen interest which every healthy man takes in healthy life, and is compounded, it seems to me, chiefly of three elements: variety, hope of creation, and the self-respect which comes of a sense of usefulness; to which must be added that mysterious bodily pleasure which goes with the deft exercise of the bodily powers. I do not think I need spend many words in trying to prove that these things, if they really and fully accompanied labour, would do much to make it pleasant. As to the pleasures of variety, any of you who have ever made anything, I don't care what, will well remember the pleasure that went with the turning out of the first specimen. What would have become of that pleasure if you had been compelled to go on making it exactly the same for ever? As to the hope of creation, the hope of producing some worthy or even excellent work which without you, the craftsman, would not have existed at all, a thing which needs you and can have no substitute for you in the making of it—can we any of us fail to understand the pleasure of this? No less easy, surely, is it to see how much the self-respect born of the consciousness of usefulness must sweeten labour. To feel that you have to do a thing not to satisfy the whim of a fool or a set of fools, but because it is really good in itself, that is useful, would surely be a good help to getting through the day's work. As to the unreasoning, sensuous pleasure in handiwork, I believe in good sooth that it has more power of getting rough and strenuous work out of men, even as things go, than most people imagine. At any rate it lies at the bottom of the production of all art, which cannot exist without it even in its feeblest and rudest form.

Now this compound pleasure in handiwork I claim as the birthright of all workmen. I say that if they lack any part of it they will be so far degraded, but that if they lack it altogether they are, so far as their work goes, I will not say slaves, the word would not be strong enough, but machines more or less conscious of their own unhappiness.

I have appealed already to history in aid of my hopes for a change in the system of the conditions of labour. I wish to bring forward now the witness of history that this claim of labour for pleasure rests on a foundation stronger than a mere fantastic dream; what is left of the art of all kinds produced in all periods and countries where hope of progress was alive before the development of the commercial system shows plainly enough to those who have eyes and understanding that pleasure did always in some degree accompany its production. This fact, however difficult it may be to demonstrate in a pedantic way, is abundantly admitted by those who have studied the arts widely; the very phrases so common in criticism that such and such a piece of would-be art is done mechanically, or done without feeling, express accurately enough the general sense of artists of a standard deduced from times of healthy art; for this mechanical and feelingless handiwork did not exist till days comparatively near our own, and it is the condition of labour under plutocratic rule which has allowed it any place at all.

The craftsman of the Middle Ages no doubt often suffered grievous material oppression, yet in spite of the rigid line of separation drawn by the hierarchical system under which he lived between him and his feudal superior, the difference between them was arbitrary rather than real; there was no such gulf in language, manners, and ideas as divides a cultivated middle-class person of to-day, a "gentleman," from even a respectable lower-class man; the mental qualities necessary to an artist, intelligence, fancy, imagination, had not then to go through the mill of the competitive market, nor had the rich (or successful competitors) made good their claim to be the sole possessors of mental refinement.

As to the conditions of handiwork in those days, the crafts were drawn together into gilds which indeed divided the occupations of men rigidly enough, and guarded the door to those occupations jealously; but as outside among the gilds there was little competition in the markets, wares being made in the first instance for domestic consumption, and only the overplus of what was wanted at home close to the place of production ever coming into the market or requiring anyone to come and go between the producer and consumer, so inside the gilds there was but little division of labour; a man or youth once accepted as an apprentice to a craft learned it from end to end, and became as a matter of course the master of it; and in the earlier days of the gilds, when the masters were scarcely ever small capitalists, there was no grade in the craft save this temporary one. Later on, when the masters became capitalists in a sort, and the apprentices were, like the masters, privileged, the class of journeymen-craftsmen came into existence; but it does not seem that the difference between them and the aristocracy of the gild was anything more than an arbitrary one. In short, during all this period the unit of labour was an intelligent man. Under this system of handiwork no great pressure of speed was put on a man's work, but he was allowed to carry it through leisurely and thoughtfully; it used the whole of a man for the production of a piece of goods, and not small portions of many men; it developed the workman's whole intelligence according to his capacity, instead of concentrating his energy on one-sided dealing with a trifling piece of work; in short, it did not submit the hand and soul of the workman to the necessities of the competitive market, but allowed them freedom for due human development. It was this system, which had not learned the lesson that man was made for commerce, but supposed in its simplicity that commerce was made for man, which produced the art of the Middle Ages, wherein the harmonious co-operation of free intelligence was carried to the furthest point which has yet been attained, and which alone of all art can claim to be called Free. The effect of this freedom, and the widespread or rather universal sense of beauty to which it gave birth, became obvious enough in the outburst of the expression of splendid and copious genius which marks the Italian Renaissance. Nor can it be doubted that this glorious art was the fruit of the five centuries of free popular art which preceded it, and not of the rise of commercialism which was contemporaneous with it; for the glory of the Renaissance faded out with strange rapidity as commercial competition developed, so that about the end of the seventeenth century, both in the intellectual and the decorative arts, the commonplace or body still existed, but the romance or soul of them was gone. Step by step they had faded and sickened before the advance of commercialism, now speedily gathering force throughout civilization. The domestic or architectural arts were becoming (or become) mere toys for the competitive market through which all material wares used by civilized men now had to pass. Commercialism had by this time well-nigh destroyed the craft-system of labour, in which, as aforesaid, the unit of labour is a fully instructed craftsman, and had supplanted it by what I will ask leave to call the workshop-system, wherein, when complete, division of labour in handiwork is carried to the highest point possible, and the unit of manufacture is no longer a man, but a group of men, each member of which is dependent on his fellows, and is utterly useless by himself. This system of the workshop division of labour was perfected during the eighteenth century by the efforts of the manufacturing classes, stimulated by the demands of the ever-widening markets; it is still the system in some of the smaller and more domestic kinds of manufacture, holding much the same place amongst us as the remains of the craft-system did in the days when that of the workshop was still young. Under this system, as I have said, all the romance of the arts died out, but the commonplace of them flourished still; for the idea that the essential aim of manufacture is the making of goods still struggled with a newer idea which has since obtained complete victory, namely, that it is carried on for the sake of making a profit for the manufacturer on the one hand, and on the other for the employment of the working classes.

This idea of commerce being an end in itself and not a means merely, being but half developed in the eighteenth century, the special period of the workshop-system, some interest could still be taken in those days in the making of wares. The capitalist-manufacturer of the period had some pride in turning out goods which would do him credit, as the phrase went; he was not willing wholly to sacrifice his pleasure in this kind to the imperious demands of commerce; even his workman, though no longer an artist, that is a free workman, was bound to have skill in his craft, limited though it was to the small fragment of it which he had to toil at day by day for his whole life.

But commerce went on growing, stimulated still more by the opening up of new markets, and pushed on the invention of men, till their ingenuity produced the machines which we have now got to look upon as necessities of manufacture, and which have brought about a system the very opposite to the ancient craft-system; that system was fixed and conservative of methods; there was no real difference in the method of making a piece of goods between the time of Pliny and the time of Sir Thomas More; the method of manufacture, on the contrary, in the present time, alters not merely from decade to decade, but from year to year; this fact has naturally helped the victory of this machine-system, the system of the Factory, where the machine-like workmen of the workshop period are supplanted by actual machines, of which the operatives (as they are now called) are but a portion, and a portion gradually diminishing both in importance and numbers. This system is still short of its full development, therefore to a certain extent the workshop-system is being carried on side by side with it, but it is being speedily and steadily crushed out by it; and when the process is complete, the skilled workman will no longer exist, and his place will be filled by machines directed by a few highly trained and very intelligent experts, and tended by a multitude of people, men, women, and children, of whom neither skill nor intelligence is required.

This system, I repeat, is as near as may be the opposite of that which produced the popular art which led up to that splendid outburst of art in the days of the Italian Renaissance which even cultivated men will sometimes deign to notice nowadays; it has therefore produced the opposite of what the old craft-system produced, the death of art and not its birth; in other words the degradation of the external surroundings of life, or simply and plainly unhappiness. Through all society spreads that curse of unhappiness: from the poor wretches, the news of whom we middle-class people are just now receiving with such naif wonder and horror: from those poor people whom nature forces to strive against hope, and to expend all the divine energy of man in competing for something less than a dog's lodging and a dog's food, from them up to the cultivated and refined person, well lodged, well fed, well clothed, expensively educated, but lacking all interest in life except, it may be, the cultivation of unhappiness as a fine art.

Something must be wrong then in art, or the happiness of life is sickening in the house of civilization. What has caused the sickness? Machine-labour will you say? Well, I have seen quoted a passage from one of the ancient Sicilian poets rejoicing in the fashioning of a water-mill, and exulting in labour being set free from the toil of the hand-quern in consequence; and that surely would be a type of a man's natural hope when foreseeing the invention of labour-saving machinery as 'tis called; natural surely, since though I have said that the labour of which art can form a part should be accompanied by pleasure, no one could deny that there is some necessary labour even which is not pleasant in itself, and plenty of unnecessary labour which is merely painful. If machinery had been used for minimizing such labour, the utmost ingenuity would scarcely have been wasted on it; but is that the case in any way? Look round the world, and you must agree with John Stuart Mill in his doubt whether all the machinery of modern times has lightened the daily work of one labourer. And why have our natural hopes been so disappointed? Surely because in these latter days, in which as a matter of fact machinery has been invented, it was by no means invented with the aim of saving the pain of labour. The phrase labour-saving machinery is elliptical, and means machinery which saves the cost of labour, not the labour itself, which will be expended when saved on tending other machines. For a doctrine which, as I have said, began to be accepted under the workshop-system, is now universally received, even though we are yet short of the complete development of the system of the Factory. Briefly, the doctrine is this, that the essential aim of manufacture is making a profit; that it is frivolous to consider whether the wares when made will be of more or less use to the world so long as any one can be found to buy them at a price which, when the workman engaged in making them has received of necessaries and comforts as little as he can be got to take, will leave something over as a reward to the capitalist who has employed him. This doctrine of the sole aim of manu-facture (or indeed of life) being the profit of the capitalist and the occupation of the workman, is held, I say, by almost everyone; its corollary is, that labour is necessarily unlimited, and that to attempt to limit it is not so much foolish as wicked, whatever misery may be caused to the community by the manufacture and sale of the wares made.

It is this superstition of commerce being an end in itself, of man made for commerce, not commerce for man, of which art has sickened; not of the accidental appliances which that superstition when put in practice has brought to its aid; machines and railways and the like, which do now verily control us all, might have been controlled by us, if we had not been resolute to seek profit and occupation at the cost of establishing for a time that corrupt and degrading anarchy which has usurped the name of Society. It is my business here to-night and everywhere to foster your discontent with that anarchy and its visible results; for indeed I think it would be an insult to you to suppose that you are contented with the state of things as they are; contented to see all beauty vanish from our beautiful city, for instance; contented with the squalor of the black country, with the hideousness of London, the wen of all wens, as Cobbett called it; contented with the ugliness and baseness which everywhere surround the life of civilized man; contented, lastly, to be living above that unutterable and sickening misery of which a few details are once again reaching us as if from some distant unhappy country, of which we could scarcely expect to hear, but which I tell you is the necessary foundation on which our society, our anarchy, rests.

Neither can I doubt that every one here has formed some idea of remedies for these defects in our civilization, as we euphemistically call them, even though the ideas be vague; also I know that you are familiar with the precepts of the system of economy, that religion, I may say, which has supplanted the precepts of the old religions on the duty and blessing of giving to the needy; you understand of course that though a friend may give to a friend and both giver and receiver be better for the gift, yet a rich man cannot give to a poor one without both being the worse for it; I suppose because they are not friends. And amidst all this I feel sure, I say, that you all of you have some ideal of a state of things better than that amidst which we live, something, I mean to say, more than the application of temporary palliatives to the enduring defects of our civilization.

Now it seems to me that the ideal of better times which the more advanced in opinion of our own class have formed as possible and hopeful is something like this. There is to be a large class of industrious people not too much refined (or they could not do the rough work wanted of them), who are to live in comfort (not, however, meaning our middle-class comfort), and receive a kind of education (if they can), and not be overworked; that is, not overworked for a working man; his light day's work would be rather heavy for the refined classes. This class is to be the basis of society, and its existence will leave the consciences of the refined class quite free and at rest. From this refined class will come the directors or captains of labour (in other words the usurers), the directors of people's consciences, religious and literary (clergy, philosophers, newspaper-writers), and lastly, if that be thought of at all, the directors of art; these two classes with or without a third, the functions of which are indefinite, will live together with the greatest goodwill, the upper helping the lower without sense of condescension on one side or humiliation on the other; the lower are to be perfectly content with their position, and there is to be no grain of antagonism between the classes: although (even Utopianism of this kind being unable to shake off the idea of the necessity of competition between individuals) the lower class, blessed and respected as it is to be, will have moreover the additional blessing of hope held out to it; the hope of each man rising into the upper class, and leaving the chrysalis of labour behind him; nor, if that matters, is the lower class to lack due political or parliamentary power; all men (or nearly all) being equal before the ballot-box, except so far as they may be bought like other things. That seems to me to be the middle-class liberal ideal of reformed society; all the world turned bourgeois, big and little, peace under the rule of competitive commerce, ease of mind, a good conscience to all and several under the rule of the devil take the hindmost.

Well, for my part I have nothing, positively nothing, to say against it if it can be brought about. Religion, morality, art, literature, science, might for all I know flourish under it and make the world a heaven. But have we not tried it somewhat already? Are not many people jubilant whenever they stand on a public platform over the speedy advent of this good time? It seems to me that the continued and advancing prosperity of the working classes is almost always noted when a political man addresses an audience on general subjects, when he forgets party politics; nor seldom when he remembers them most. Nor do I wish to take away honour where honour is due; I believe there are many people who deeply believe in the realization of this ideal while they are not ignorant of how lamentably far things are from it at present; I know that there are men who sacrifice time, money, pleasure, their own prejudices even, to bring it about; men who hate strife and love peace, men hard working, kindly, unambitious. What have they done? How much nearer are they to the ideal of the bourgeois commonwealth than they were at the time of the Reform Bill, or the time of the repeal of the Corn Laws? Well, thus much nearer to a great change perhaps, that there is a chink in the armour of self-satisfaction; a suspicion that perhaps it is not the accidents of the system of competitive commerce which have to be abolished, but the system itself; but as to approaching the ideal of that system reformed into humanity and decency, they are about so much nearer to it as a man is nearer to the moon when he stands on a hayrick. I don't want to make too much of the matter of money-wages apart from the ghastly contrast between the rich and the poor which is the essence of our system; yet remember that poverty driven below a certain limit means degradation and slavery pure and simple. Now I have seen a statement made by one of the hopeful men of the rich middle class that the average yearly income of an English working man's household is one hundred pounds. I don't believe the figures because I am sure that they are swollen by wages paid in times of inflation, and ignore the precarious position of most working men; but quite apart from that, do not, I beg you, take refuge behind averages; for at least they are swelled by the high wages paid to special classes of workmen in special places, and in the manufacturing districts by the mothers of families working in factories, to my mind a most abominable custom, and by other matters of the like kind, which the average makers leave you to find out for yourselves. But even that is not the point of the matter. For my part the enormous average of one hundred pounds a year to so many millions of toiling people, while many thousands who do not toil think themselves poor with ten times the income, does not comfort me for the fact of a thousand strong men waiting at the dock gates down at Poplar the greater part of a working-day, on the chance of some of them being taken on at wretched wages, or for the ordinary wage of a farm labourer over a great part of England being then shillings per week, and that considered ruinous by the farmers also: if averages will content us while such things as this go on, why stop at the working classes? Why not take in everybody, from the Duke of Westminster downwards, and then raise a hymn of rejoicing over the income of the English people?

I say let us be done with averages and look at lives and their sufferings, and try to realize them: for indeed what I want you to note is this; that though you may realize a part of the bourgeois or radical ideal, there is and for ever will be under the competitive system a skeleton in the cupboard. We may, nay, we have managed to create a great mass of middling well-to-do people, hovering on the verge of the middle classes, prosperous artisans, small tradesmen, and the like; and I must say parenthetically that in spite of all their innate good qualities the class does little credit to our civilization; for though they live in a kind of swinish comfort as far as food is concerned, they are ill housed, ill educated, crushed by grovelling superstitions, lacking reasonable pleasures, utterly devoid of any sense of beauty. But let that pass. For aught I know we may very much increase the proportionate numbers of this class, without making any serious change in our system, but under all that still lies and will lie another class which we shall never get rid of as long as we are under the tyranny of the devil take the hindmost; that class is the Class of Victims. Now above all things I want us not to forget them (as indeed we are not likely to for some weeks to come), or to console ourselves by averages for the fact that the riches of the rich and the comfort of the well-to-do are founded on that terrible mass of undignified, unrewarded, useless misery, concerning which we have of late been hearing a little, a very little; after all we do know that is a fact, and we can only console ourselves by hoping that we may, if we are watchful and diligent (which we very seldom are), we may greatly diminish the amount of it. I ask you, is such a hope as that worthy of our boasted civilization with its perfected creeds, its high morality, its sounding political maxims? Will you think it monstrous that some people have conceived another hope, and see before them the ideal of a society in which there should be no classes permanently degraded for the benefit of the commonweal? For one thing I would have you remember, that this lowest class of utter poverty lies like a gulf before the whole of the working classes, who in spite of all averages live a precarious life; the failure in the game of life which entails on a rich man an unambitious retirement, and on a well-to-do man a life of dependence and laborious shifts, drags a working man down into that hell of irredeemable degradation. I hope there are but few, at least here, who can comfort their consciences by saying that the working classes bring this degradation on themselves by their own unthrift and recklessness. Some do, no doubt, stoic philosophers of the higher type not being much commoner among day-labourers than among the well-to-do and rich; but we know very well how sorely the mass of the poor strive, practising such thrift as is in itself a degradation to man, in whose very nature it is to love mirth and pleasure, and how in spite of all that they fall into the gulf. What! are we going to deny that when we see all round us in our own class cases of men failing in life by no fault of their own; nay, many of the failers worthier and more useful than those that succeed: as might indeed be looked for in the state of war which we call the system of unlimited competition, where the best campaigning-luggage a man can carry is a hard heart and no scruples? For indeed the fulfilment of that liberal ideal of the reform of our present system into a state of moderate class supremacy is impossible, because that system is after all nothing but a continuous implacable war; the war once ended, commerce, as we now understand the word, comes to an end, and the mountains of wares which are either useless in themselves or only useful to slaves and slave-owners are no longer made, and once again art will be used to determine what things are useful and what useless to be made; since nothing should be made which does not give pleasure to the maker and the user, and that pleasure of making must produce art in the hands of the workman. So will art be used to discriminate between the waste and the usefulness of labour; whereas at present the waste of labour is, as I have said above, a matter never considered at all; so long as a man toils he is supposed to be useful, no matter what he toils at.

I tell you the very essence of competitive commerce is waste; the waste that comes of the anarchy of war. Do not be deceived by the outside appearance of order in our plutocratic society. It fares with it as it does with the older forms of war, that there is an outside look of quiet wonderful order about it; how neat and comforting the steady march of the regiment; how quiet and respectable the sergeants look; how clean the polished cannon; neat as a new pin are the storehouses of murder; the books of adjutant and sergeant as innocent-looking as may be; nay, the very orders for destruction and plunder are given with a quiet precision which seems the very token of a good conscience;

79

this is the mask that lies before the ruined cornfield and the burning cottage, the mangled bodies, the untimely death of worthy men, the desolated home. All this, the results of the order and sobriety which is the face which civilized soldiering turns towards us stay-at-homes, we have been told often and eloquently enough to consider; often enough we have been shown the wrong side of the glories of war, nor can we be shown it too often or too eloquently. Yet I say even such a mask is worn by competitive commerce, with its respectable prim order, its talk of peace and the blessings of intercommunication of countries and the like; and all the while its whole energy, its whole organized precision is employed in one thing, the wrenching the means of living from others; while outside that everything must do as it may, whoever is the worse or the better for it; as in the war of fire and steel, all other aims must be crushed out before that one object. It is worse than the older war in one respect at least, that whereas that was intermittent, this is continuous and unresting, and its leaders and captains are never tired of declaring that it must last as long as the world, and is the end-all and be-all of the creation of man and of his home. Of such the words are said:

> For them alone do seethe
> A thousand men in troubles wide and dark;
> Half ignorant they turn an easy wheel
> That sets sharp racks at work to pinch and peel.

What can overthrow this terrible organization so strong in itself, so rooted in the self-interest, stupidity, and cowardice of strenuous narrow-minded men; so strong in itself and so much fortified against attack by the surrounding anarchy which it has bred? Nothing but discontent with that anarchy, and an order which in its turn will arise from it, nay, is arising from it; an order once a part of the internal organization of that which it is doomed to destroy. For the fuller development of industrialism from the ancient crafts through the workshop-system into the system of the factory and machine, while it has taken from the work-men all pleasure in their labour, or hope of distinction and excellence in it, has welded them into a great class, and has by its very oppression and compulsion of the monotony of life driven them into feeling the solidarity of their interests and the antagonism of those interests to those of the capitalist class; they are all through civilization feeling the necessity of their rising as a class. As I have said, it is impossible for them to coalesce with the middle classes to produce the universal reign of moderate bourgeois society which some have dreamed of; because however many of them may rise out of their class, these become at once part of the middle class, owners of capital, even though it be in a small way, and exploiters of labour; and there is still left behind a lower class which in its own turn drags down to it the unsuccessful in the struggle; a process which is being accelerated in these latter days by the rapid growth of the great factories and stores, which are extinguishing the remains of the small workshops served by men who may hope to become small masters, and also the smaller of the tradesman class. Thus then, feeling that it is impos-sible for them to rise as a class, while competition naturally, and as a necessity for its existence, keeps them down, they have begun to look to association as their natural tendency, just as competition is looked to by the capitalists; in them the hope has arisen, if nowhere else, of finally making an end of class degradation.

It is in the belief that this hope is spreading to the middle classes that I stand before you now, pleading for its accept-ance by you, in the certainty that in its fulfilment alone lies the other hope for the new birth of Art and the attainment by the middle classes of true refinement, the lack of which at present is so grievously betokened by the sordidness and baseness of all the external surroundings of our lives, even those of us who are rich. I know there are some to whom this possibility of the getting rid of class degradation may come, not as a hope, but as a fear. These may comfort themselves by thinking that this Socialist matter is a hollow scare, in England at least; that the proletariat have no hope, and therefore will lie quiet in this country, where the rapid and nearly complete development of commercialism has crushed the power of combination out of the lower classes; where the very combinations, the Trades Unions, founded for the advancement of the working class as a class, have already become conservative and obstructive bodies, wielded by the middle-class politicians for party purposes; where the proportion of the town and manufacturing districts to the country is so great that the inhabitants, no longer recruited by the peasantry but become townsmen bred of townsmen, are yearly deteriorating in physique; where lastly education is so backward.

It may be that in England the mass of the working classes has no hope; that it will not be hard to keep them down for a while, possibly a long while. The hope that this may be so I will say plainly is a dastard's hope, for it is founded on the chance of their degradation. I say such an expectation is that of slave-holders or the hangers-on of slave-holders. I believe, however, that hope is growing among the working classes even in England; at any rate you may be sure of one thing, that there is at least discontent. Can any of us doubt that, since there is unjust suffering? Or which of us would be contented with ten shillings a week to keep our households with, or to dwell in unutterable filth and have to pay the price of good lodging for it? Do you doubt that if we had any time for it amidst our struggle to live we should look into the title of those who kept us there, themselves rich and comfortable, under the pretext that it was necessary to society? I tell you there is plenty of discontent, and I call on all those who think there is something better than making money for the sake of making it to help in educating that discontent into hope, that is into the demand for the new birth of society; and I do this not because I am afraid of it, but because I myself am discontented and long for justice.

Yet, if any of you are afraid of the discontent which is abroad, in its present shape, I cannot say that you have no reason to be. I am representing reconstructive Socialism before you; but there are other people who call themselves Socialists whose aim is not reconstruction, but destruction; people who think that the present state of things is horrible and unbearable (as in very truth it is), and that there is nothing for it but to shake society by constant blows given at any sacrifice, so that it may at last totter and fall. May it not be worth while, think you, to combat such a doctrine by supplying discontent with hope of change that involves reconstruction? Meanwhile, be sure that, though the day of change may be long delayed, it will come at last. The middle classes will one day become conscious of the discontent of the proletariat; before that some will have renounced their class and cast in their lot with the working men, influenced by love of justice or insight into facts. For the rest, they will, when their conscience is awakened, have two choices before them; they must either cast aside their morality, of which though three parts are cant, the other is sincere, or they must give way. In either case I do believe that the change will come, and that nothing will seriously retard that new birth; yet I well know that the middle class may do much to give a peaceable or a violent character to the education of discontent which must precede it. Hinder it, and who knows what violence you may be driven into, even to the renunciation of the morality of which we middle-class men are so proud; advance it, strive single-heartedly that truth may prevail, and what need you fear? At any rate not your own violence, not your own tyranny?

Again I say things have gone too far, and the pretence at least of a love of justice is too common among us, for the middle classes to attempt to keep the proletariat in its condition of slavery to capital, as soon as they stir seriously in the matter, except at the cost of complete degradation to themselves, the middle class, whatever else may happen. I cannot help hoping that there are some here who are already in dread of the shadow of that degradation of consciously sustaining an injustice, and are eager to escape from that half-ignorant tyranny of which Keats tells, and which is, sooth to say, the common condition of rich people. To those I have a last word or two to say in begging them to renounce their class pretensions and cast in their lot with the working men. It may be that some of them are kept from actively furthering the cause which they believe in by that dread of organization, by that unpracticality in a word, which, as it is very common in England generally, is more common among highly cultivated people, and, if you will forgive the word, most common in our ancient universities. Since I am a member of a Socialist propaganda I earnestly beg those of you who agree with me to help us actively, with your time and your talents if you can, but if not, at least with your money, as you can. Do not hold aloof from us, since you agree with us, because we have not attained that delicacy of manners, that refinement of language, nay, even that prudent and careful wisdom of action which the long oppression of competitive commerce has crushed out of us.

Art is long and life is short; let us at least do something before we die. We seek perfection, but can find no perfect means to bring it about; let it be enough for us if we can unite with those whose aims are right, and their means honest and feasible. I tell you if we wait for perfection in association in these days of combat we shall die before we can do anything. Help us now, you whom the fortune of your birth has helped to make wise and refined; and as you help us in our work-a-day business toward the success of the cause, instil into us your superior wisdom, your superior refinement, and you in your turn may be helped by the courage and hope of those who are not so completely wise and refined. Remember we have but one weapon against that terrible organization of selfishness which we attack, and that weapon is Union. Yes, and it should be obvious union, which we can be conscious of as we mix with others who are hostile or indiffernt to the cause; organized brotherhood is that which must break the spell of anarchical Plutocracy. One man with an idea in his head is in danger of being considered a madman; two men with the same idea in common may be foolish, but can hardly be mad; ten men sharing an idea begin to act, a hundred draw attention as fanatics, a thousand and society begins to tremble, a hundred thousand and there is war abroad, and the cause has victories tangible and real; and why only a hundred thousand? Why not a hundred million and peace upon the earth? You and I who agree together, it is we who have to answer that question.

USEFUL WORK VERSUS USELESS TOIL

[Delivered before the Hampstead Liberal Club on January 16th, 1884, and repeated five days later in Manchester. First published as a Socialist League pamphlet, 1885. *Collected Works*, XXIII, 98-120, Cole, 603-23, Jackson, 175-93.

This is one of Morris' most popular and often repeated lectures. It is notable for his clear explanation of capitalist exploitation and for the detailed statement of his position about the role of machinery—much more positive than he is often credited with.]

THE above title may strike some of my readers as strange. It is assumed by most people nowadays that all work is useful, and by most *well-to-do* people that all work is desirable. Most people, well-to-do or not, believe that, even when a man is doing work which appears to be useless, he is earning his livelihood by it—he is "employed", as the phrase goes; and most of those who are well-to-do cheer on the happy worker with congratulations and praises, if he is only "industrious" enough and deprives himself of all pleasure and holidays in the sacred cause of labour. In short, it has become an article of the creed of modern morality that all labour is good in itself—a convenient belief to those who live on the labour of others. But as to those on whom they live, I recommend them not to take it on trust, but to look into the matter a little deeper.

Le us grant, first, that the race of man must either labour or perish. Nature does not give us our livelihood gratis; we must win it by toil of some sort or degree. Let us see, then, if she does not give us some compensation for this compulsion to labour, since certainly in other matters she takes care to make the acts necessary to the continuance of life in the individual and the race not only endurable, but even pleasurable.

You may be sure that she does so, that it is of the nature of man, when he is not diseased, to take pleasure in his work under certain conditions. And, yet, we must say in the teeth of the hypocritical praise of all labour, whatsoever it may be, of which I have made mention, that there is some labour which is so far from being a blessing that it is a curse; that it would be better for the community and for the worker if the latter were to fold his hands and refuse to work, and either die or let us pack him off to the workhouse or prison — which you will.

Here, you see, are two kinds of work—one good, the other bad; one not far removed from a blessing, a lightening of life; the other a mere curse, a burden to life.

What is the difference between them, then? This: one has hope in it, the other has not. It is manly to do the one kind of work, and manly also to refuse to do the other.

What is the nature of the hope which, when it is present in work, makes it worth doing?

It is threefold, I think — hope of rest, hope of product, hope of pleasure in the work itself; and hope of these also in some abundance and of good quality; rest enough and good enough to be worth having; product worth having by one who is neither a fool nor an ascetic; pleasure enough for all for us to be conscious of it while we are at work; not a mere habit, the loss of which we shall feel as a fidgety man feels the loss of the bit of string he fidgets with.

I have put the hope of rest first because it is the simplest and most natural part of our hope. Whatever pleasure there is in some work, there is certainly some pain in all work, the beast-like pain of stirring up our slumbering energies to action, the beast-like dread of change when things are pretty well with us; and the compensation for this animal pain in animal rest. We must feel while we are working that the time will come when we shall not have to work. Also the rest, when it comes, must be long enough to allow us to enjoy it; it must be longer than is merely necessary for us to recover the strength we have expended in working, and it must be animal rest also in this, that it must not be disturbed by anxiety, else we shall not be able to enjoy it. If we have this amount and kind of rest we shall, so far, be no worse off than the beasts.

As to the hope of product, I have said that Nature compels us to work for that. It remains for *us* to look to it that we *do* really produce something, and not nothing, or at least nothing that we want or are allowed to use. If we look to this and use our wills we shall, so far, be better than machines.

The hope of pleasure in the work itself: how strange that hope must seem to some of my readers—to most of them! Yet I think that to all living things there is a pleasure in the exercise of their energies, and that even beasts rejoice in being lithe and swift and strong. But a man at work, making something which he feels will exist because he is working at it and wills it, is exercising the energies of his mind and soul as well as of his body. Memory and imagination help him as he works. Not only his own thoughts, but the thoughts of the men of past ages guide his hands; and, as a part of the human race, he creates. If we work thus we shall be men, and our days will be happy and eventful.

Thus worthy work carries with it the hope of pleasure in rest, the hope of the pleasure in our using what it makes, and the hope of pleasure in our daily creative skill.

All other work but this is worthless; it is slaves' work—mere toiling to live, that we may live to toil.

Therefore, since we have, as it were, a pair of scales in which to weigh the work now done in the world, let us use them. Let us estimate the worthiness of the work we do, after so many thousand years of toil, so many promises of hope deferred, such boundless exultation over the progress of civilization and the gain of liberty.

Now, the first thing as to the work done in civilization and the easiest to notice is that it is portioned out very unequally amongst the different classes of society. First, there are people—not a few—who do no work, and make no pretence of doing any. Next, there are people, and very many of them, who work fairly hard, though with abundant easements and holidays, claimed and allowed; and lastly, there are people who work so hard that they may be said to do nothing else than work, and are accordingly called " the working classes," as distinguished from the middle classes and the rich, or aristocracy, whom I have mentioned above.

It is clear that this inequality presses heavily upon the "working" class, and must visibly tend to destroy their hope of rest at least, and so, in that particular, make them worse off than mere beasts of the field; but that is not the sum and end of our folly of turning useful work into useless toil, but only the beginning of it.

For first, as to the class of rich people doing no work, we all know that they consume a great deal while they produce nothing. Therefore, clearly, they have to be kept at the expense of those who do work, just as paupers have, and are a mere burden on the community. In these days there are many who have learned to see this, though they can see no further into the evils of our present system, and have formed no idea of any scheme for getting rid of this burden; though perhaps they have a vague hope that changes in the system of voting for members of the House of Commons, may, as if by magic, tend in that direction. With such hopes or superstitions we need not trouble ourselves. Moreover, this class, the aristocracy, once thought most necessary to the State, is scant of numbers, and has now no power of its own, but depends on the support of the class next below it—the middle class. In fact, it is really composed either of the most successful men of that class, or of their immediate descendants.

As to the middle class, including the trading, manufacturing, and professional people of our society, they do, as a rule, seem to work quite hard enough, and so at first sight might be thought to help the community, and not burden it. But by far the greater part of them, though they work, do not produce, and even when they do produce, as in the case of those engaged (wastefully indeed) in the distribution of goods, or doctors, or (genuine) artists and literary men, they consume out of all proportion to their due share. The commercial and manufacturing part of them, the most powerful part, spend their lives and energies in fighting amongst themselves for their respective shares of the wealth which they *force* the genuine workers to provide for them; the others are almost wholly the hangers-on of these; they do not work for the public, but a privileged class; they are the parasites of property, sometimes, as in the case of lawyers, undisguisedly so; sometimes, as the doctors and others above mentioned, professing to be useful, but too often of no use save as supporters of the system of folly, fraud, and tyranny of which they form a part. And all these we must remember have, as a rule, one aim in view; not the production of utilities, but the gaining of a position either for themselves or their children in which they will not have to work at all. It is their ambition and the end of their whole lives to gain, if not for themselves yet at least for their children, the proud position of being obvious burdens on the community. For their work itself, in spite of the sham dignity with which they surround it, they care nothing: save a few enthusiasts, men of science, art or letters, who, if they are not the salt of the earth, are at least (and, oh, the pity of it!) the salt of the miserable system of which they are the slaves, which hinders and thwarts them at every turn and even sometimes corrupts them.

Here then is another class, this time very numerous and all-powerful, which produces very little and consumes enormously, and is therefore in the main supported, as paupers are, by the real producers. The class that remains to be considered produces all that is produced, and supports both itself and the other classes, though it is placed in a position of inferiority to them; real inferiority, mind you, involving a degradation both of mind and body. But it is a necessary consequence of this tyranny and folly that again many of these workers are not producers. A vast number of them once more are merely parasites of property, some of them openly so, as the soldiers by land and sea who are kept on foot for the perpetuating of national rivalries and enmities, and for the purposes of the national struggle for the share of the product of unpaid labour. But besides this obvious burden on the producers and the scarcely less obvious one of domestic servants, there is first the army of clerks, shop-assistants, and so forth, who are engaged in the service of the private war for wealth, which, as above said, is the real occupation of the well-to-do middle class. This is a larger body of workers than might be supposed, for it includes amongst others all those engaged in what I should call competitive salesmanship, or, to use a less dignified word, the puffery of wares, which has now got to such a pitch that there are many things which cost far more to sell than they do to make.

Next there is the mass of people employed in making all those articles of folly and luxury, the demand for which is the outcome of the existence of the rich non-producing classes; things which people leading a manly and uncorrupted life would not ask for or dream of. These things, whoever may gainsay me, I will for ever refuse to call wealth: they are not wealth, but waste. Wealth is what Nature gives us and what a reasonable man can make out of the gifts of Nature for his reasonable use. The sunlight, the fresh air, the unspoiled face of the earth, food, raiment and housing necessary and decent; the storing up of knowledge of all kinds, and the power of disseminating it; means of free communication between man and man; works of art, the beauty which man creates when he is most a man, most aspiring and thoughtful—all things which serve the pleasure of people, free, manly and uncorrupted This is wealth. Nor can I think of anything worth having which does not come under one or other of these heads. But think, I beseech you, of the product of England, the workshop of the world, and will you not be bewildered, as I am, at the tought of the mass of things which no sane man could desire, but which our useless toil makes — and sells?

Now, further, there is even a sadder industry yet, which is forced on many, very many, of our workers—the making of wares which are necessary to them and their brethren, *because they are an inferior class.* For if many men live without producing, nay, must live lives so empty and foolish that they *force* a great part of the workers to produce wares which no one needs, not even the rich, it follows that most men must be poor; and, living as they do on wages from those whom they support, cannot get for their use the *goods* which men naturally desire, but must put up with miserable makeshifts for them, with coarse food that does not nourish, with rotten raiment which does not shelter, with wretched houses which may well make a town-dweller in civilization look back with regret to the tent of the nomad tribe, or the cave of the pre-historic savage. Nay, the workers must even lend a hand to the great industrial invention of the age — adulteration, and by its help produce for their own use shams and mockeries of the luxury of the rich; for the wage-earners must always live as the wage-payers bid them, and their very habits of life are *forced* on them by their masters.

But it is waste of time to try to express in words due contempt of the productions of the much praised cheapness of our epoch. It must be enough to say that this cheapness is necessary to the system of exploiting on which modern manufacture rests. In other words, our society includes a great mass of slaves, who must be fed, clothed, housed and amused as slaves, and that their daily necessity compels them to make the slave-wares whose use is the perpetuation of their slavery.

To sum up, then, concerning the manner of work in

civilized States, these States are composed of three classes—a class which does not even pretend to work, a class which pretends to work but which produces nothing, and a class which works, but is compelled by the other two classes to do work which is often unproductive.

Civilization therefore wastes its own resources, and will do so as long as the present system lasts. These are cold words with which to describe the tyranny under which we suffer; try then to consider what they mean.

There is a certain amount of natural material and of natural forces in the world, and a certain amount of labour-power inherent in the persons of the men that inhabit it. Men urged by their necessities and desires have laboured for many thousands of years at the task of subjugating the forces of Nature and of making the natural material useful to them. To our eyes, since we cannot see into the future, that struggle with Nature seems nearly over, and the victory of the human race over her nearly complete. And, looking backwards to the time when history first began, we note that the progress of that victory has been far swifter and more startling within the last two hundred years than ever before. Surely, therefore, we moderns ought to be in all ways vastly better off than any who have gone before us. Surely we ought, one and all of us, to be wealthy, to be well furnished with the good things which our victory over Nature has won for us.

But what is the real fact? Who will dare to deny that the great mass of civilized men are poor? So poor are they that it is mere childishness troubling ourselves to discuss whether perhaps they are in some ways a little better off than their forefathers. They are poor; nor can their poverty be measured by the poverty of a resourceless savage, for he knows of nothing else than his poverty; that he should be cold, hungry, houseless, dirty, ignorant, all that is to him as natural as that he should have a skin. But for us, for the most of us, civilization has bred desires which she forbids us to satisfy, and so is not merely a niggard but a torturer also.

Thus then have the fruits of our victory over Nature been stolen from us, thus has compulsion by Nature to labour in hope of rest, gain, and pleasure been turned into compulsion by man to labour in hope—of living to labour!

What shall we do then, can we mend it?

Well, remember once more that it is not our remote ancestors who achieved the victory over Nature, but our fathers, nay, our very selves. For us to sit hopeless and helpless then would be a strange folly indeed: be sure that we can amend it. What, then, is the first thing to be done?

We have seen that modern society is divided into two classes, one of which is *privileged* to be kept by the labour of the other—that is, it forces the other to work for it and takes from this inferior class everything that it *can* take from it, and uses the wealth so taken to keep its own members in a superior position, to make them beings of a higher order than the others: longer lived, more beautiful, more honoured, more refined than those of the other class. I do not say that it troubles itself about its members being *positively* long lived, beautiful or refined, but merely insists that they shall be so *relatively* to the inferior class. As also it cannot use the labour-power of the inferior class fairly in producing real wealth, it wastes it wholesale in the production of rubbish.

It is this robbery and waste on the part of the minority which keeps the majority poor; if it could be shown that it is necessary for the preservation of society that this should be submitted to, litte more could be said on the matter, save that the despair of the oppressed majority would probably at some time or other destroy Society. But it has been shown, on the contrary, even by such incomplete experiments, for instance, as Co-operation (so called), that the existence of a privileged class is by no means necessary for the production of wealth, but rather for the "government" of the producers of wealth, or, in other words, for the upholding of privilege.

The first step to be taken then is to abolish a class of

men privileged to shirk their duties as men, thus forcing others to do the work which they refuse to do. All must work according to their ability, and so produce what they consume—that is, each man should work as well as he can for his own livelihood, and his livelihood should be assured to him; that is to say, all the advantages which society would provide for each and all of its members.

Thus, at last, would true Society be founded. It would rest on equality of condition. No man would be tormented for the benefit of another—nay, no one man would be tormented for the benefit of Society. Nor, indeed, can that order be called Society which is not upheld for the benefit of every one of its members.

But since men live now, badly as they live, when so many people do not produce at all, and when so much work is wasted, it is clear that, under conditions where all produced and no work was wasted, not only would every one work with the certain hope of gaining a due share of wealth by his work, but also he could not miss his due share of rest. Here, then, are two out of the three kinds of hope mentioned above as an essential part of worthy work assured to the worker. When class robbery is abolished, every man will reap the fruits of his labour, every man will have due rest—leisure, that is. Some Socialists might say we need not go any further than this; it is enough that the worker should get the full produce of his work, and that his rest should be abundant. But though the compulsion of man's tyranny is thus abolished, I yet demand compensation for the compulsion of Nature's necessity. As long as the work is repulsive it will still be a burden which must be taken up daily, and even so would mar our life, even though the hours of labour were short. What we want to do is to add to our wealth without diminishing our pleasure. Nature will not be finally conquered till our work becomes a part of the pleasure of our lives.

That first step of freeing people from the compulsion to labour needlessly will at least put us on the way towards this happy end; for we shall then have time and opportunities for bringing it about. As things are now, between the waste of labour-power in mere idleness and its waste in unproductive work, it is clear that the world of civilization is supported by a small part of its people; when *all* were working *usefully* for its support, the share of work which each would have to do would be but small, if our standard of life were about on the footing of what well-to-do and refined people now think desirable. We shall have labour-power to spare, and shall in short, be as wealthy as we please. It will be easy to live. If we were to wake up some morning now, under our present system, and find it "easy to live," that system would force us to set to work at once and make it hard to live; we should call that "developing our resources," or some such fine name. The multiplication of labour has become a necessity for us, and as long as that goes on no ingenuity in the invention of machines will be of any real use to us. Each new machine will cause a certain amount of misery among the workers whose special industry it may disturb; so many of them will be reduced from skilled to unskilled workmen, and then gradually matters will slip into their due grooves, and all will work apparently smoothly again; and if it were not that all this is preparing revolution, things would be, for the greater part of men, just as they were before the new wonderful invention.

But when revolution has made it "easy to live," when all are working harmoniously together and there is no one to rob the worker of his time, that is to say, his life; in those coming days there will be no compulsion on us to go on producing things we do not want, no compulsion on us to labour for nothing; we shall be able calmly and thoughtfully to consider what we shall do with our wealth of labour-power. Now, for my part, I think the first use we ought to make of that wealth, of that freedom, should be to make all our labour, even the commonest and most necessary, pleasant to everybody; for thinking over the matter carefully I can see that the one course which will certainly make life happy in the face of all accidents and troubles is to take a pleasurable interest in all the details of life. And lest perchance you think that an assertion too universally accepted to be worth making, let me remind you how entirely modern civilization forbids it; with what sordid, and even terrible, details it surrounds the life of the poor, what a mechanical and empty life she forces on the rich; and how rare a holiday it is for any of us to feel ourselves a part of Nature, and unhurriedly, thoughtfully, and happily to note the course of our lives amidst all the little links of events which connect them with the lives of others, and build up the great whole of humanity.

But such a holiday our whole lives might be, if we were resolute to make all our labour reasonable and pleasant. But we must be resolute indeed; for no half measures will help us here. It has been said already that our present joyless labour, and our lives scared and anxious as the life of a hunted beast, are forced upon us by the present system of producing for the profit of the privileged classes. It is necessary to state what this means. Under the present system of wages and capital the "manufacturer" (most absurdly so called, since a manufacturer means a person who makes with his hands) having a monopoly of the means whereby the power to labour inherent in every man's body can be used for production, is the master of those who are not so privileged; he, and he alone, is able to make use of this labour-power, which, on the other hand, is the only commodity by means of which his "capital," that is to say the accumulated product of past labour, can be made productive to him. He therefore buys the labour-power of those who are bare of capital and can only live by selling it to him; his purpose in this transaction is to increase his capital, to make it breed. It is clear that if he paid those with whom he makes his bargain the full value of their labour, that is to say, all that they produced, he would fail in his purpose. But since he is the monopolist of the means of productive labour, he can *compel* them to make a bargain better for him and worse for them than that; which bargain is that after they have earned their livelihood, estimated according to a standard high enough to ensure their peaceable submission to his mastership, the rest (and by far the larger part as a matter of fact) of what they produce shall belong to him, shall be his *property* to do as he likes with, to use or abuse at his pleasure; which property is, as we all know, jealously guarded by army and navy, police and prison; in short, by that huge mass of physical force which superstition, habit, fear of death by starvation—Ignorance, in one word, among the propertyless masses enables the propertied classes to use for the subjection of—their slaves.

Now, at other times, other evils resulting from this system may be put forward. What I want to point out now is the impossibility of our attaining to attractive labour under this system, and to repeat that it is this robbery (there is no other word for it) which wastes the available labour-power of the civilized world, forcing many men to do nothing, and many, very many more to do nothing useful; and forcing those who carry on really useful labour to most burdensome overwork. For understand once for all that the "manufacturer" aims primarily at producing, by means of the labour he has stolen from others, not goods but profits, that is, the "wealth" that is produced over and above the livelihood of his workmen, and the wear and tear of his machinery. Whether that "wealth" is real or sham matters nothing to him. If it sells and yields him a "profit" it is all right. I have said that, owing to there being rich people who have more money than they can spend reasonably, and who therefore buy sham wealth, there is waste on that side; and also that, owing to there being poor people who cannot afford to buy things which are worth making, there is waste on that side. So that the "demand" which the capitalist "supplies" is a false demand. The market in which he sells is "rigged" by the miserable inequalities produced by the robbery of the system of Capital and Wages.

It is this system, therefore, which we must be resolute in getting rid of, if we are to attain to happy and useful work for all. The first step towards making labour attractive is to get the means of making labour fruitful, the Capital, including the land, machinery, factories, etc., into the hands of the community, to be used for the good of all alike, so that we might all work at "supplying" the real "demands" of each and all—that is to say, work for livelihood, instead of working to supply the demand of the profit market—instead of working for profit—i.e., the power of compelling other men to work against their will.

When this first step has been taken and men begin to understand that Nature wills all men either to work or starve, and when they are no longer such fools as to allow some the alternative of stealing, when this happy day is come, we shall then be relieved from the tax of waste, and consequently shall find that we have, as aforesaid, a mass of labour-power available, which will enable us to live as we please within reasonable limits. We shall no longer be hurried and driven by the fear of starvation, which at present presses no less on the greater part of men in civilized communities than it does on mere savages. The first and most obvious necessities will be so easily provided for in a community in which there is no waste of labour, that we shall have time to look round and consider what we really do want, that can be obtained without over-taxing our energies; for the often expressed fear of mere idleness falling upon us when the force supplied by the present hierarchy of compulsion is withdrawn, is a fear which is but generated by the burden of excessive and repulsive labour, which we most of us have to bear at present.

I say once more that, in my belief, the first thing which we shall think so necessary as to be worth sacrificing some idle time for, will be the attractiveness of labour. No very heavy sacrifice will be required for attaining this object, but some *will* be required. For we may hope that men who have just waded through a period of strife and revolution will be the last to put up long with a life of mere utilitarianism, though Socialists are sometimes accused by ignorant persons of aiming at such a life. On the other hand, the ornamental part of modern life is already rotten to the core, and must be utterly swept away before the new order of things is realized. There is nothing of it—there is nothing which could come of it that could satisfy the aspirations of men set free from the tyranny of commercialism.

We must begin to build up the ornamental part of life—its pleasures, bodily and mental, scientific and artistic, social and individual—on the basis of work undertaken willingly and cheerfully, with the consciousness of benefiting ourselves and our neighbours by it. Such absolutely necessary work as we should have to do would in the first place take up but a small part of each day, and so far would not be burdensome; but it would be a task of daily recurrence, and therefore would spoil our day's pleasure unless it were made at least endurable while it lasted. In other words, all labour, even the commonest, must be made attractive.

How can this be done?—is the question the answer to which will take up the rest of this paper. In giving some hints on this question, I know that, while all Socialists will agree with many of the suggestions made, some of them may seem to some strange and venturesome. These must be considered as being given without any intention of dogmatizing, and as merely expressing my own personal opinion.

From all that has been said already it follows that labour, to be attractive, must be directed towards some obviously useful end, unless in cases where it is undertaken voluntarily by each individual as a pastime. This element of obvious usefulness is all the more to be counted on in sweetening tasks otherwise irksome, since social morality, the responsibility of man towards the life of man, will, in the new order of things, take the place of theological morality, the responsibility of man to some abstract idea. Next, the day's work will be short. This need not be insisted on. It is clear that with work unwasted it *can* be short. It is clear also that much work which is now a torment, would be easily endurable if it were much shortened.

Variety of work is the next point, and a most important

one. To compel a man to do day after day the same task, without any hope of escape or change, means nothing short of turning his life into a prison-torment. Nothing but the tyranny of profit-grinding makes this necessary. A man might easily learn and practise at least three crafts, varying sedentary occupation with outdoor—occupation calling for the exercise of strong bodily energy for work in which the mind had more to do. There are few men, for instance, who would not wish to spend part of their lives in the most necessary and pleasantest of all work— cultivating the earth. One thing which will make this variety of employment possible will be the form that education will take in a socially ordered community. At present all education is directed towards the end of fitting people to take their places in the hierarchy of commerce—these as masters, those as workmen. The education of the masters is more ornamental than that of the workmen, but it is commercial still; and even at the ancient universities learning is but little regarded, unless it can in the long run be made to *pay*. Due education is a totally different thing from this, and concerns itself in finding out what different people are fit for, and helping them along the road which they are inclined to take. In a duly ordered society, therefore, young people would be taught such handicrafts as they had a turn for as a part of their education, the discipline of their minds and bodies; and adults would also have opportunities of learning in the same schools, for the development of individual capacities would be of all things chiefly aimed at by education, instead, as now, the subordination of all capacities to the great end of "money-making" for oneself— or one's master. The amount of talent, and even genius, which the present system crushes, and which would be drawn out by such a system, would make our daily work easy and interesting.

Under this head of variety I will note one product of industry which has suffered so much from commercialism that it can scarcely be said to exist, and is, indeed, so foreign from our epoch that I fear there are some who will find it difficult to understand what I have to say on the subject, which I nevertheless must say, since it is really a most important one. I mean that side of art which is, or ought to be, done by the ordinary workman while he is about his ordinary work, and which has got to be called, very properly, Popular Art. This art, I repeat, no longer exists now, having been killed by commercialism. But from the beginning of man's contest with Nature till the rise of the present capitalistic system, it was alive, and generally flourished. While it lasted, everything that was made by man was adorned by man, just as everything made by Nature is adorned by her. The craftsman, as he fashioned the thing he had under his hand, ornamented it so naturally and so entirely without conscious effort, that it is often difficult to distinguish where the mere utilitarian part of his work ended and the ornamental began. Now the origin of this art was the necessity that the workman felt for variety in his work, and though the beauty produced by this desire was a great gift to the world, yet the obtaining variety and pleasure in the work by the workman was a matter of more importance still, for it stamped all labour with the impress of pleasure. All this has now quite disappeared from the work of civilization. If you wish to have ornament, you must pay specially for it, and the workman is compelled to produce ornament, as he is to produce other wares. He is compelled to pretend happiness in his work, so that the beauty produced by man's hand, which was once a solace to his labour, has now become an extra burden to him, and ornament is now but one of the follies of useless toil, and perhaps not the least irksome of its fetters.

Besides the short duration of labour, its conscious usefulness, and the variety which should go with it, there is another thing needed to make it attractive, and that is pleasant surroundings. The misery and squalor which we people of civilization bear with so much complacency as a necessary part of the manufacturing system, is just as necessary to the community at large as a proportionate amount of filth would be in the house of a private rich man. If such a man were to allow the cinders to be raked all over his drawing-room, and a privy to be established in each corner of his dining-room, if he habitually made a dust and refuse heap of his once beautiful garden, never washed his sheets or changed his tablecloth, and made his family sleep five in a bed, he would surely find himself in the claws of a commission *de lunatico*. But such acts of miserly folly are just what our present society is doing daily under the compulsion of a supposed necessity, which is nothing short of madness. I beg you to bring your commission of lunacy against civilization without more delay.

For all our crowded towns and bewildering factories are simply the outcome of the profit system. Capitalistic manufacture, capitalistic land-owning, and capitalistic exchange force men into big cities in order to manipulate them in the interests of capital; the same tyranny contracts the due space of the factory so much that (for instance) the interior of a great weaving-shed is almost as ridiculous a spectacle as it is a horrible one. There is no other necessity for all this, save the necessity for grinding profits out of men's lives, and of producing cheap goods for the use (and subjection) of the slaves who grind. All labour is not yet driven into factories; often where it is there is no necessity for it, save again the profit-tyranny. People engaged in all such labour need by no means be compelled to pig together in close city quarters. There is no reason why they should not follow their occupations in quiet country homes, in industrial colleges, in small towns, or, in short, where they find it happiest for them to live.

As to that part of labour which must be associated on a large scale, this very factory system, under a reasonable order of things (though to my mind there might still be drawbacks to it), would at least offer opportunities for a full and eager social life surrounded by many pleasures. The factories might be centres of intellectual activity also, and work in them might well be varied very much: the tending of the necessary machinery might to each individual be but a short part of the day's work. The other work might vary from raising food from the surrounding country to the study and practice of art and science. It is a matter of course that people engaged in such work, and being the masters of their own lives, would not allow any hurry or want of foresight to force them into enduring dirt, disorder, or want of room. Science duly applied would enable them to get rid of refuse, to minimize, if not wholly to destroy, all the inconveniences which at present attend the use of elaborate machinery, such as smoke, stench and noise; nor would they endure that the buildings in which they worked or lived should be ugly blots on the fair face of the earth. Beginning by making their factories, buildings, and sheds decent and convenient like their homes, they would infallibly go on to make them not merely negatively good, inoffensive merely, but even beautiful, so that the glorious art of architecture, now for some time slain by commercial greed, would be born again and flourish.

So, you see, I claim that work in a duly ordered community should be made attractive by the consciousness of usefulness, by its being carried on with intelligent interest, by variety, and by its being exercised amidst pleasurable surroundings. But I have also claimed, as we all do, that the day's work should not be wearisomely long. It may be said, "How can you make this last claim square with the others? If the work is to be so refined, will not the goods made be very expensive?"

I do admit, as I have said before, that some sacrifice will be necessary in order to make labour attractive. I mean that, if we *could* be contented in a free community to work in the same hurried, dirty, disorderly, heartless way as we do now, we might shorten our day's labour very much more than I suppose we shall do, taking all kinds of labour into account. But if we did, it would mean that our new-won freedom of condition would leave us listless and wretched, if not anxious, as we are now, which I hold is simply impossible. We should be contented to make the sacrifices necessary for raising our condition to the standard called out for as desirable by the whole community.

Nor only so. We should, individually, be emulous to sacrifice quite freely still more of our time and our ease towards the raising of the standard of life. Persons, either by themselves or associated for such purposes, would freely, and for the love of the work and for its results—stimulated by the hope of the pleasure of creation—produce those ornaments of life for the service of all, which they are now bribed to produce (or pretend to produce) for the service of a few rich men. The experiment of a civilized community living wholly without art or literature has not yet been tried. The past degradation and corruption of civilization may force this denial of pleasure upon the society which will arise from its ashes. If that must be, we will accept the passing phase of utilitarianism as a foundation for the art which is to be. If the cripple and the starveling disappear from our streets, if the earth nourish us all alike, if the sun shine for all of us alike, if to one and all of us the glorious drama of the earth—day and night, summer and winter—can be presented as a thing to understand and love, we can afford to wait awhile till we are purified from the shame of the past corruption, and till art arises again amongst people freed from the terror of the slave and the shame of the robber.

Meantime, in any case, the refinement, thoughtfulness, and deliberation of labour must indeed be paid for, but not by compulsion to labour long hours. Our epoch has invented machines which would have appeared wild dreams to the men of past ages, and of those machines we have as yet *made no use*.

They are called "labour-saving" machines—a commonly used phrase which implies what we expect of them; but we do not get what we expect. What they really do is to reduce the skilled labourer to the ranks of the unskilled, to increase the number of the "reserve army of labour"—that is, to increase the precariousness of life among the workers and to intensify the labour of those who serve the machines (as slaves their masters). All this they do by the way, while they pile up the profits of the employers of labour, or force them to expend those profits in bitter commercial war with each other. In a true society these miracles of ingenuity would be for the first time used for minimizing the amount of time spent in unattractive labour, which by their means might be so reduced as to be but a very light burden on each individual. All the more as these machines would most certainly be very much improved when it was no longer a question as to whether their improvement would "pay" the individual, but rather whether it would benefit the community.

So much for the ordinary use of machinery, which would probably, after a time, be somewhat restricted when men found out that there was no need for anxiety as to mere subsistence, and learned to take an interest and pleasure in handiwork which, done deliberately and thoughtfully, could be made more attractive than machine work.

Again, as people freed from the daily terror of starvation find out what they really wanted, being no longer compelled by anything but their own needs, they would refuse to produce the mere inanities which are now called luxuries, or the poison and trash now called cheap wares. No one would make plush breeches when there were no flunkies to wear them, nor would anybody waste his time over making oleomargarine when no one was *compelled* to abstain from real butter. Adulteration laws are only needed in a society of thieves—and in such a society they are a dead letter.

Socialists are often asked how work of the rougher and more repulsive kind could be carried out in the new condition of things. To attempt to answer such questions fully or authoritatively would be attempting the impossibility of constructing a scheme of a new society out of the materials of the old, before we knew which of those materials would disappear and which endure through the evolution which is leading us to the great change. Yet it is not difficult to conceive of some arrangement whereby those who did the roughest work should work for the shortest spells. And again, what is said above of the variety of work applies specially here. Once more I say, that for a man to be the whole of his life hopelessly engaged in performing one repulsive and never-ending task, is an arrangement fit enough for the hell imagined by theologians, but scarcely fit for any other form of society. Lastly, if this rougher work were of any special kind, we may suppose that special volunteers would be called on to perform it, who would surely be forthcoming, unless men in a state of freedom should lose the sparks of manliness which they possessed as slaves.

And yet if there be any work which cannot be made other than repulsive, either by the shortness of its duration or the intermittency of its recurrence, or by the sense of special and peculiar usefulness (and therefore honour) in the mind of the man who performs it freely—if there be any work which cannot be but a torment to the worker, what then? Well, then, let us see if the heavens will fall on us if we leave it undone, for it were better that they should. The produce of such work cannot be worth the price of it.

Now we have seen that the semi-theological dogma that all labour, under any circumstances, is a blessing to the labourer, is hypocritical and false; that, on the other hand, labour is good when due hope of rest and pleasure accompanies it. We have weighed the work of civilization in the balance and found it wanting, since hope is mostly lacking to it, and therefore we see that civilization has bred a dire curse for men. But we have seen also that the work of the world might be carried on in hope and with pleasure if it were not wasted by folly and tyranny, by the perpetual strife of opposing classes.

It is Peace, therefore, which we need in order that we may live and work in hope and with pleasure. Peace so much desired, if we may trust men's words, but which has been so continually and steadily rejected by them in deeds. But for us, let us set our hearts on it and win it at whatever cost.

What the cost may be, who can tell? Will it be possible

to win peace peaceably? Alas, how can it be? We are so hemmed in by wrong and folly, that in one way or other we must always be fighting against them: our own lives may see no end to the struggle, perhaps no obvious hope of the end. It may be that the best we can hope to see is that struggle getting sharper and bitterer day by day, until it breaks out openly at last into the slaughter of men by actual warfare instead of by the slower and crueller methods of "peaceful" commerce. If we live to see that, we shall live to see much; for it will mean the rich classes grown conscious of their own wrong and robbery, and consciously defending them by open violence; and then the end will be drawing near.

But in any case, and whatever the nature of our strife for peace may be, if we only aim at it steadily and with singleness of heart, and ever keep it in view, a reflection from that peace of the future will illumine the turmoil and trouble of our lives, whether the trouble be seemingly petty, or obviously tragic; and we shall, in our hopes at least, live the lives of men: nor can the present times give us any reward greater than that.

ART AND SOCIALISM

[A lecture delivered before the Leicester Secular Society on January 23rd, 1884. First published as a pamphlet at Leek, 1884. *Collected Works*, XXIII, 192-214, Cole, 624-45, Jackson, 96-114.

Its outstanding feature is perhaps the stress laid on work as a necessity of human life, not merely as a means of obtaining a livelihood. Morris insists that only Socialism can restore work to its proper, central position.]

MY friends, I want you to look into the relations of Art to Commerce, using the latter word to express what is generally meant by it; namely, that system of competition in the market which is indeed the only form which most people now-a-days suppose that Commerce can take.

Now whereas there have been times in the world's history when Art held the supremacy over Commerce; when Art was a good deal, and Commerce, as we understand the word, was a very little; so now on the contrary it will be admitted by all, I fancy, that Commerce has become of very great importance and Art of very little.

I say this will be generally admitted, but different persons will hold very different opinions not only as to whether this is well or ill, but even as to what it really means when we say that Commerce has become of supreme importance and that Art has sunk into an unimportant matter.

Allow me to give you my opinion of the meaning of it; which will lead me on to ask you to consider what remedies should be applied for curing the evils that exist in the relations between Art and Commerce.

Now to speak plainly it seems to me that the supremacy of Commerce (as we understand the word) is an evil, and a very serious one; and I should call it an unmixed evil—but for the strange continuity of life which runs through all historical events, and by means of which the very evils of such and such a period tend to abolish themselves.

For to my mind it means this: that the world of modern civilization in its haste to gain a very inequitably divided material prosperity has entirely suppressed popular Art: or in other words that the greater part of the people have no share in Art—which as things now are must be kept in the hands of a few rich or well-to-do people, who we may fairly say need it less and not more than the laborious workers.

Nor is that all the evil, nor the worst of it; for the cause of this famine of Art is that whilst people work throughout the civilized world as laboriously as ever they did, they have lost—in losing an Art which was done by and for the people—the natural solace of that labour; a solace which they once had, and always should have, the opportunity of expressing their own thoughts to their fellows by means of that very labour, by means of that daily work which nature or long custom, a second nature, does indeed require of them, but without meaning that it should be an unrewarded and repulsive burden.

But, through a strange blindness an error in the civilization of these latter days, the world's work almost all of it—the work some share of which should have been the helpful companion of every man—has become even such a burden, which every man, if he could, would shake off. I have said that people work no less laboriously than they ever did; but I should have said that they work more laboriously.

The wonderful machines which in the hands of just and foreseeing men would have been used to minimize repulsive labour and to give pleasure—or in other words added life—to the human race, have been so used on the contrary that they have driven all men into mere frantic haste and hurry, thereby destroying pleasure, that is life, on all hands: they have instead of lightening the labour of the workmen, intensified it, and thereby added more weariness yet to the burden which the poor have to carry.

Nor can it be pleaded for the system of modern civilization that the mere material or bodily gains of it balance the loss of pleasure which it has brought upon the world; for as I hinted before those gains have been so unfairly divided that the contrast between rich and poor has been fearfully intensified, so that in all civilized countries, but most of all in England, the terrible spectacle is exhibited of two peoples, living street by street, and door by door—people of the same blood, the same tongue, and at least nominally living under the same laws—but yet one civilized and the other uncivilized.

All this I say is the result of the system that has trampled down Art, and exalted Commerce into a sacred religion; and it would seem is ready, with the ghastly stupidity which is its principal characteristic, to mock the Roman satirist for his noble warning by taking it in inverse meaning, and now bids us all "for the sake of life to destroy the reasons for living."

And now in the teeth of this stupid tyranny I put forward a claim on behalf of labour enslaved by Commerce, which I know no thinking man can deny is reasonable, but which if acted on would involve such a change as would defeat Commerce; that is, would put Association instead of Competition, Social order instead of Individualist anarchy.

Yet I have looked at this claim by the light of history and my own conscience, and it seems to me so looked at to be a most just claim, and that resistance to it means nothing short of a denial of the hope of civilization.

This then is the claim:—

It is right and necessary that all men should have work to do which shall be worth doing, and be of itself pleasant to do; and which should be done under such conditions as would make it neither over-wearisome nor over-anxious.

Turn that claim about as I may, think of it as long as

I can, I cannot find that it is an exorbitant claim; yet again I say if Society would or could admit it, the face of the world would be changed; discontent and strife and dishonesty would be ended. To feel that we were doing work useful to others and pleasant to ourselves, and that such work and its due reward *could* not fail us! What serious harm could happen to us then? And the price to be paid for so making the world happy is Revolution: Socialism instead of *laissez-faire*.

How can we of the middle classes help to bring such a state of things about; a state of things as nearly as possible the reverse of the present state of things?

The reverse; no less than that. For first, *The work must be worth doing*: think what a change that would make in the world! I tell you I feel dazed at the thought of the immensity of work which is undergone for the making of useless things.

It would be an instructive day's work for any one of us who is strong enough to walk through two or three of the principal streets of London on a week-day, and take accurate note of everything in the shop windows which is embarrassing or superfluous to the daily life of a serious man. Nay, the most of these things no one, serious or unserious, wants at all; only a foolish habit makes even the lightest-minded of us suppose that he wants them, and to many people even of those who buy them they are obvious encumbrances to real work, thought and pleasure. But I beg you to think of the enormous mass of men who are occupied with this miserable trumpery, from the engineers who have had to make the machines for making them, down to the hapless clerks who sit day-long year after year in the horrible dens wherein the wholesale exchange of them is transacted, and the shopmen, who not daring to call their souls their own, retail them amidst numberless insults which they must not resent, to the idle public which doesn't want them but buys them to be bored by them and sick to death of them.

I am talking of the merely useless things; but there are

other matters not merely useless, but actively destructive and poisonous which command a good price in the market; for instance, adulterated food and drink. Vast is the number of slaves whom competitive Commerce employs in turning out infamies such as these. But quite apart from them there is an enormous mass of labour which is just merely wasted; many thousands of men and women making *nothing* with terrible and inhuman toil which deadens the soul and shortens mere animal life itself.

All these are the slaves of what is called luxury, which in the modern sense of the word comprises a mass of sham wealth, the invention of competitive Commerce, and enslaves not only the poor people who are compelled to work at its production, but also the foolish and not overhappy people who buy it to harass themselves with its encumbrance.

Now if we are to have popular Art, or indeed Art of any kind, we must at once and for all be done with this *luxury;* it is the supplanter, the changeling of Art; so much so that by those who know of nothing better it has even been taken for Art, the divine solace of human labour, the romance of each day's hard practice of the difficult art of living.

But I say Art cannot live beside it, nor self-respect in any class of life. Effeminacy and brutality are its companions on the right hand and the left. This, first of all, we of the well-to-do classes must get rid of if we are serious in desiring the new birth of Art: and if not then corruption is digging a terrible pit of perdition for society, from which indeed the new birth may come, but surely from amidst of terror, violence and misery.

Indeed if it were but ridding ourselves, the well-to-do people, of this mountain of rubbish that would be something worth doing: things which everybody knows are of no use; the very capitalists know well that there is no genuine healthy demand for them, and they are compelled to foist them off on the public by stirring up a strange feverish desire for petty excitement, the outward token of which is known by the conventional name of fashion—a strange monster born of the vacancy of the lives of rich people, and the eagerness of competitive Commerce to make the most of the huge crowd of workmen whom it breeds as unregarded instruments for what is called the making of money.

Do not think it a little matter to resist this monster of folly; to think for yourselves what you yourselves really desire, will not only make men and women of you so far, but may also set you thinking of the due desires of other people, since you will soon find when you get to know a work of Art, that slavish work is *un*desirable.

And here furthermore is at least a little sign whereby to distinguish between a rag of fashion and a work of Art: whereas the toys of fashion when the first gloss is worn off them do become obviously worthless even to the frivolous—a work of Art, be it ever so humble, is long lived; we never tire of it; as long as a scrap hangs together it is valuable and instructive to each new generation. All works of Art in short have the property of becoming venerable amidst decay: and reason good, for from the first there was a soul in them, the thought of man, which will be visible in them so long as the body exists in which they were implanted.

And that last sentence brings me to considering the other side of the necessity for labour only occupying itself in making goods that are worth making. Hitherto we have been thinking of it only from the user's point of view; even so looked at it was surely important enough; yet from the other side—as to the producer—it is far more important still.

For I say again that in buying these things

'Tis the lives of men you buy!

Will you from mere folly and thoughtlessness make yourselves partakers of the guilt of those who compel their fellow men to labour uselessly?

For when I said it was necessary for all things made to

be worth making, I set up that claim chiefly on behalf of *Labour;* since the waste of making useless things grieves the workman doubly. As part of the public he is *forced* into buying them, and the more part of his miserable wages are squeezed out of him by an universal kind of truck system; as one of the producers he is *forced* into making them, and so into losing the very foundations of that pleasure in daily work which I claim as his birthright; he is compelled to labour joylessly at making the poison which the truck system compels him to buy. So that the huge mass of men who are compelled by folly and greed to make harmful and useless things are sacrificed to Society. I say that this would be terrible and unendurable even though they were sacrificed to the good of Society—if that were possible; but if they are sacrificed not for the welfare of Society but for its whims, to add to its degradation, what do luxury and fashion look like then? On one side ruinous and wearisome waste leading through corruption to corruption on to complete cynicism at last, and the disintegration of all Society; and on the other side—implacable oppression destructive of all pleasure and hope in life, and leading—whitherward?

Here then is one thing for us of the middle classes to do before we can clear the ground for the new birth of Art, before we can clear our own consciences of the guilt of enslaving men by their labour. One thing; and if we *could* do it perhaps that one thing would be enough, and all other healthy changes would follow it; but can we do it? Can we escape from the corruption of Society which threatens us? Can the middle classes regenerate themselves?

At first sight one would say that a body of people so powerful, who have built up the gigantic edifice of modern Commerce, whose science, invention and energy have subdued the forces of nature to serve their every-day purposes, and who guide the organization that keeps these natural powers in subjection in a way almost miraculous; at first sight one would say surely such a mighty mass of wealthy men could do anything they please.

And yet I doubt it: their own creation, the Commerce they are so proud of, has become their master; and all we of the well-to-do classes—some of us with triumphant glee, some with dull satisfaction, and some with sadness of heart—are compelled to admit not that Commerce was made for man, but that man was made for Commerce.

On all sides we are forced to admit it. There are of the English middle class to-day, for instance, men of the highest aspirations towards Art, and of the strongest will; men who are most deeply convinced of the necessity to civilization of surrounding men's lives with beauty; and many lesser men, thousands for what I know, refined and cultivated, follow them and praise their opinions: but both the leaders and the led are incapable of saving so much as half a dozen commons from the grasp of inexorable Commerce: they are as helpless in spite of their culture and their genius as if they were just so many overworked shoemakers: less lucky than King Midas, our green fields and clear waters, nay the very air we breathe are turned not to gold (which might please some of us for an hour may be) but to dirt; and to speak plainly we know full well that under the present gospel of Capital not only there is no hope of bettering it, but that things grow worse year by year, day by day. Let us eat and drink, for to-morrow we die—choked by filth.

Or let me give you a direct example of the slavery to competitive Commerce, in which we hapless folk of the middle classes live. I have exhorted you to the putting away of luxury, to the stripping yourselves of useless encumbrances, to the simplification of life, and I believe that there are not a few of you that heartily agree with me on that point. Well, I have long thought that one of the most revolting circumstances that cling to our present class-system, is the relation between us, of the well-to-do, and our domestic servants: we and our servants live together under one roof, but are little better than strangers to each other, in spite of the good nature and good feeling that often exists on both sides: nay strangers is a mild word;

though we are of the same blood, bound by the same laws, we live together like people of different tribes. Now think how this works on the job of getting through the ordinary day's work of a household, and whether our lives can be simplified while such a system lasts. To go no further, you who are housekeepers know full well (as I myself do, since I have learned the useful art of cooking a dinner) how it would simplify the day's work, if the chief meals could be eaten in common; if there had not got to be double meals, one upstairs, another down stairs. And again, surely we of this educational century, cannot be ignorant of what an education it would be for the less refined members of a household to meet on common easy terms the more refined once a day, at least; to note the elegant manners of well-bred ladies, to give and take in talk with learned and travelled men, with men of action and imagination: believe me that would beat elementary education.

Furthermore this matter cleaves close to our subject of Art: for note, as a token of this stupidity of our sham civilization, what foolish rabbit warrens our well-to-do houses are obliged to be; instead of being planned in the rational ancient way which was used from the time of Homer to past the time of Chaucer, a big hall, to wit, with a few chambers tacked on to it for sleeping or sulking in. No wonder our houses are cramped and ignoble when the lives lived in them are cramped and ignoble also.

Well, and why don't we who have thought of this, as I am sure many of us have, change this mean and shabby custom, simplifying our lives thereby and educating our *friends*, to whose toil we owe so many comforts? Why do not you—and I—set about doing this to-morrow?

Because we *cannot;* because our servants wouldn't have it, knowing, as we know, that both parties would be made miserable by it.

The civilization of the nineteenth century forbids us to share the refinement of a household among its members!

So you see, if we middle-class people belong to a powerful

folk, and in good sooth we do, we are but playing a part played in many a tale of the world's history: we are great but hapless; we are important dignified people, but bored to death; we have bought our power at price of our liberty and our pleasure.

So I say in answer to the question Can we put luxury from us and live simple and decent lives? Yes, when we are free from the slavery of Capitalist Commerce; but not before.

Surely there are some of you who long to be free; who have been educated and refined, and had your perceptions of beauty and order quickened only that they might be shocked and wounded at every turn, by the brutalities of competitive Commerce; who have been so hunted and driven by it that, though you are well-to-do, rich even may be, you have now nothing to lose from social revolution: love of Art, that is to say of the true pleasure of life, has brought you to this, that you must throw in your lot with that of the wage-slave of competitive Commerce; you and he must help each other and have one hope in common, or you at any rate will live and die hopeless and unhelped. You who long to be set free from the oppression of the money grubbers, hope for the day when you will be *compelled* to be free!

Meanwhile if otherwise that oppression has left scarce any work to do worth doing, one thing at least is left us to strive for, the raising of the standard of life where it is lowest, where it is low: that will put a spoke in the wheel of the triumphant car of competitive Commerce.

Nor can I conceive of anything more likely to raise the standard of life than the convincing some thousands of those who live by labour, of the necessity of their supporting the second part of the claim I have made for Labour; namely *That their work should be of itself pleasant to do.* If we could but convince them that such a strange revolution in Labour as this would be of infinite benefit not to them only, but to all men; and that it is so right and natural that for the reverse to be the case, that most men's work should be grievous to them, is a mere monstrosity of these latter days, which must in the long run bring ruin and confusion on the Society that allows it—If we could but convince them, then indeed there would be chance of the phrase *Art of the People* being something more than a mere word.

At first sight, indeed, it would seem impossible to make men born under the present system of Commerce understand that labour may be a blessing to them: not in the sense in which the phrase is sometimes preached to them by those whose labour is light and easily evaded: not as a necessary task laid by nature on the poor for the benefit of the rich; not as an opiate to dull their sense of right and wrong, to make them sit down quietly under their burdens to the end of time, blessing the squire and his relations: all this they could understand our saying to them easily enough, and sometimes would listen to it I fear with at least a show of complacency—if they thought there were anything to be made out of us thereby. But the true doctrine that labour should be a real tangible blessing in itself to the working man, a pleasure even as sleep and strong drink are to him now: this one might think it hard indeed for him to understand, so different as it is to anything which he has found labour to be.

Nevertheless though most men's work is only borne as a necessary evil like sickness, my experience as far as it goes is, that whether it be from a certain sacredness in handiwork which does cleave to it even under the worst circumstances, or whether it be that the poor man who is driven by necessity to deal with things which are terribly real, when he thinks at all on such matters, thinks less conventionally than the rich; whatever it may be, my experience so far is that the working man finds it easier to understand the doctrine of the claim of Labour to pleasure in the work itself than the rich or well-to-do man does. Apart from any trivial words of my own, I have been surprised to find, for instance, such a hearty feeling toward John Ruskin among working-class audiences: they can see the prophet in him rather than the fantastic rhetorician, as more superfine audiences do.

That is a good omen, I think, for the education of times to come. But we who somehow are so tainted by cynicism, because of our helplessness in the ugly world which surrounds and presses on us, cannot we somehow raise our own hopes at least to the point of thinking that what hope glimmers on the millions of the slaves of Commerce is something better than a mere delusion, the false dawn of a cloudy midnight with which 'tis only the moon that struggles? Let us call to mind that there yet remain monuments in the world which show us that all human labour was not always a grief and a burden to men. Let us think of the mighty and lovely architecture, for instance, of mediæval Europe: of the buildings raised before Commerce had put the coping stone on the edifice of tyranny by the discovery that fancy, imagination, sentiment, the joy of creation and the hope of fair fame are marketable articles too precious to be allowed to men who have not the money to buy them, to mere handicraftsmen and day labourers. Let us remember there was a time when men had pleasure in their daily work, but yet as to other matters hoped for light and freedom even as they do now: their dim hope grew brighter, and they watched its seeming fulfilment drawing nearer and nearer, and gazed so eagerly on it that they did not note how the ever watchful foe, oppression, had changed his shape and was stealing from them what they had already gained in the days when the light of their new hope was but a feeble glimmer; so they lost the old gain, and for lack of it the new gain was changed and spoiled for them into something not much better than loss.

Betwixt the days in which we now live and the end of the Middle Ages, Europe has gained freedom of thought, increase of knowledge, and huge talent for dealing with the material forces of nature; comparative political freedom withal and respect for the lives of *civilized* men, and other gains that go with these things: nevertheless I say deliberately that if the present state of Society is to endure, she has bought these gains at too high a price in the loss of the pleasure in daily work which once did certainly solace the mass of men for their fears and oppressions: the death of Art was too high a price to pay for the material prosperity of the middle classes.

Grievous indeed it was, that we could not keep both our hands full, that we were forced to spill from one while we gathered with the other: yet to my mind it is more grievous still to be unconscious of the loss; or being dimly conscious of it to have to force ourselves to forget it and to cry out that all is well.

For, though all is not well, I know that men's natures are not so changed in three centuries that we can say to all the thousands of years which went before them; You were wrong to cherish Art, and now we have found out that all men need is food and raiment and shelter, with a smattering of knowledge of the material fashion of the universe. Creation is no longer a need of man's soul, his right hand may forget its cunning, and he be none the worse for it.

Three hundred years, a day in the lapse of ages, has not changed man's nature thus utterly, be sure of that: one day we shall win back Art, that is to say the pleasure of life; win back Art again to our daily labour. Where is the hope then, you may say; Show it us.

There lies the hope, where hope of old deceived us. We gave up Art for what we thought was light and freedom, but it was less than light and freedom which we bought: the light showed many things to those of the well-to-do who cared to look for them: the freedom left the well-to-do free enough if they cared to use their freedom; but these were few at the best: to the most of men the light showed them that they need look for hope no more, and the freedom left the most of men free—to take at a wretched wage what slave's work lay nearest to them or starve.

There is our hope, I say. If the bargain had been really fair, complete all round, then were there nought else to do but to bury Art, and forget the beauty of life: but now the cause of Art has something else to appeal to: no less than the hope of the people for the happy life which has not yet been granted to them. There is our hope: the cause of Art is the cause of the people.

Think of a piece of history, and so hope! Time was when the rule of Rome held the whole world of civilization in its poisonous embrace. To all men—even the best, as you may see in the very gospels—that rule seemed doomed to last for ever: nor to those who dwelt under it was there any world worth thinking of beyond it: but the days passed and though none saw a shadow of the coming change, it came none the less, like a thief in the night, and the *Barbarians*, the world which lay outside the rule of Rome, were upon her; and men blind with terror lamented the change and deemed the world undone by the Fury of the North. But even that fury bore with it things long strange to Rome, which once had been the food its glory fed on: hatred of lies, scorn of riches, contempt of death, faith in the fair fame won by steadfast endurance, honourable love of women—all these things the Northern Fury bore with it, as the mountain torrent bears the gold; and so Rome fell and Europe rose, and the hope of the world was born again.

To those that have hearts to understand, this tale of the past is a parable of the days to come; of the change in store for us hidden in the breast of the Barbarism of civilization—the Proletariat; and we of the middle class, the strength of the mighty but monstrous system of competitive Commerce, it behoves us to clear our souls of greed and cowardice and to face the change which is now once more on the road; to see the good and the hope it bears with it amidst all its threats of violence, amidst all its ugliness, which was not born of itself but of that which it is doomed to destroy.

Now once more I will say that we well-to-do people, those of us who love Art, not as a toy, but as a thing necessary to the life of man, as a token of his freedom and happiness, have for our best work the raising of the standard of life among the people; or in other words establishing the claim I made for Labour—which I will now put in a different form, that we may try to see what chiefly hinders us from making that claim good and what are the enemies to be attacked. Thus I put the claim again:

Nothing should be made by man's labour which is not worth making; or which must be made by labour degrading to the makers.

Simple as that proposition is, and obviously right as I am sure it must seem to you, you will find, when you come to consider the matter, that it is a direct challenge to the death to the present system of labour in civilized countries. That system, which I have called competitive Commerce, is distinctly a system of war; that is of waste and destruction: or you may call it gambling if you will, the point of it being that under it whatever a man gains he gains at the expense of some other man's loss. Such a system does not and cannot heed whether the matters it makes are worth making; it does not and cannot heed whether those who make them are degraded by their work: it heeds one thing and only one, namely, what it calls making a profit; which word has got to be used so conventionally that I must explain to you what it really means, to wit the plunder of the weak by the strong! Now I say of this system, that it is of its very nature destructive of Art, that is to say of the happiness of life. Whatever consideration is shown for the life of the people in these days, whatever is done which is worth doing, is done in spite of the system and in the teeth of its maxims; and most true it is that we do, all of us, tacitly at least, admit that it is opposed to all the highest aspirations of mankind.

Do we not know, for instance, how those men of genius work who are the salt of the earth, without whom the corruption of society would long ago have become unendurable? The poet, the artist, the man of science, is it not true that in their fresh and glorious days, when they are in the heyday of their faith and enthusiasm, they are thwarted at every turn by Commercial war, with its sneering question "Will it pay?" Is it not true that when they begin to win worldly success, when they become comparatively rich, in spite of ourselves they seem to us tainted by the contact with the commercial world?

Need I speak of great schemes that hang about neglected; of things most necessary to be done, and so confessed by all men, that no one can seriously set a hand to because of the lack of money; while if it be a question of creating or stimulating some foolish whim in the public mind, the satisfaction of which will breed a profit, the money will come in by the ton. Nay, you know what an old story it is of the wars bred by Commerce in search of new markets, which not even the most peaceable of statesmen can resist; an old story and still it seems for ever new, and now become a kind of grim joke, at which I would rather not laugh if I could help it, but am even forced to laugh from a soul laden with anger.

And all that mastery over the powers of nature which the last hundred years or less has given us: what has it done for us under this system? In the opinion of John Stuart Mill, it was doubtful if all the mechanical inventions of modern times have done anything to lighten the toil of labour: be sure there is no doubt, that they were not made for that end, but to "make a profit." Those almost miraculous machines, which if orderly forethought had dealt with them might even now be speedily extinguishing all irksome and unintelligent labour, leaving us free to raise the standard of skill of hand and energy of mind in our workmen, and to produce afresh that loveliness and order which only the hand of man guided by his soul can produce—what have they done for us now? Those machines of which the civilized world is so proud, has it any right to be proud of the *use* they have been put to by Commercial war and waste?

I do not think exultation can have a place here: Commercial war has made a profit of these wonders; that is to say it has by their means bred for itself millions of unhappy workers, unintelligent machines as far as their daily work goes, in order to get cheap labour, to keep up its exciting but deadly game for ever. Indeed that labour would have been cheap enough—cheap to the Commercial war generals, and deadly dear to the rest of us—but for the seeds of freedom which valiant men of old have sowed amongst us to spring up in our own day into Chartism and Trades Unionism and Socialism, for the defence of order and a decent life. Terrible would have been our slavery, and not of the working classes alone, but for these germs of the change which must be.

Even as it is, by the reckless aggregation of machine-workers and their adjoints in the great cities and the manufacturing districts, it has kept down life amongst us, and keeps it down to a miserably low standard; so low that any standpoint for improvement is hard to think of even. By the means of speedy communication which it has created, and which should have raised the standard of life by spreading intelligence from town to country, and widely creating modest centres of freedom of thought and habits of culture—by the means of the railways and the like it has gathered to itself fresh recruits for the reserve army of competing lack-alls on which its gambling gains so much depend, stripping the country-side of its population, and extinguishing all reasonable hope and life in the lesser towns.

Nor can I, an artist, think last or least of the outward effects which betoken this rule of the wretched anarchy of Commercial war. Think of the spreading sore of London swallowing up with its loathsomeness field and wood and heath without mercy and without hope, mocking our feeble efforts to deal even with its minor evils of smoke-laden sky and befouled river: the black horror and reckless squalor of our manufacturing districts, so dreadful to the senses which are unused to them that it is ominous for the future of the race that any man can live among it in tolerable cheerfulness: nay in the open country itself the thrusting aside by miserable jerry-built brick and slate of the solid grey dwellings that are still scattered about, fit emblems in their cheery but beautiful simplicity of the yeomen of the English field, whose destruction at the hands of yet young Commercial war was lamented so touchingly by the high-minded More and the valiant Latimer. Everywhere in short the change from old to new involving one certainty, whatever else may be doubtful, a worsening of the aspect of the country.

This is the condition of England: of England the country of order, peace and stability, the land of common sense and practicality; the country to which all eyes are turned of those whose hope is for the continuance and perfection of modern progress. There are countries in Europe whose aspect is not so ruined outwardly, though they may have less of material prosperity, less wide-spread middle-class wealth to balance the squalor and disgrace I have mentioned: but if they are members of the great Commercial whole, through the same mill they have got to go, unless something should happen to turn aside the triumphant march of War Commercial before it reaches the end.

That is what three centuries of Commerce have brought that hope to which sprung up when feudalism began to fall to pieces. What can give us the day-spring of a new hope? What, save general revolt against the tyranny of Commercial war? The palliatives over which many worthy people are busying themselves now are useless: because they are but unorganized partial revolts against a vast wide-spreading grasping organization which will, with the unconscious instinct of a plant, meet every attempt at bettering the condition of the people with an attack on a fresh side; new machines, new markets, wholesale emigration, the revival of grovelling superstitions, preachments of thrift to lack-alls, of temperance to the wretched; such things as these will baffle at every turn all partial revolts against the monster we of the middle classes have created for our own undoing.

I will speak quite plainly on this matter, though I must say an ugly word in the end if I am to say what I think. The one thing to be done is to set people far and wide to think it possible to raise the standard of life. If you think of it, you will see clearly that this means stirring up *general discontent*.

And now to illustrate that I turn back to my blended claim for Art and Labour, that I may deal with the third clause in it: here is the claim again:—

It is right and necessary that all men should have work to do—
First—*Work worth doing;*
Second—*Work of itself pleasant to do;*
Third—*Work done under such conditions as would make it neither over-wearisome nor over-anxious.*

With the first and second clauses, which are very nearly related to each other, I have tried to deal already. They are as it were the soul of the claim for proper labour; the third clause is the body without which that soul cannot exist. I will extend it in this way, which will indeed partly carry us over ground already covered:

No one who is willing to work should ever fear want of such employment as would earn for him all due necessaries of mind and body.

All due necessaries—what are the due necessaries for a good citizen?

First, *honourable and fitting work*: which would involve giving him a chance of gaining capacity for his work by due education; also, as the work must be worth doing and pleasant to do, it will be found necessary to this end that his position be so assured to him that he cannot be compelled to do useless work, or work in which he cannot take pleasure.

The second necessity is *decency of surroundings*: including *(a)* good lodging; *(b)* ample space; *(c)* general order and beauty. That is (a) our houses must be well built, clean and healthy; (b) there must be abundant garden space in our towns, and our towns must not eat up the fields and natural features of the country; nay I demand even that there be left waste places and wilds in it, or romance and poetry—that is Art—will die out amongst us. (c) Order and beauty means, that not only our houses must be stoutly and properly built, but also that they be ornamented duly: that the fields be not only left for cultivation, but also that they be not spoilt by it any more than a garden is spoilt: no one for instance to be allowed to cut down, for mere profit, trees whose loss would spoil a landscape: neither on any pretext should people be allowed to darken the daylight with smoke, to befoul rivers, or to degrade any spot of earth with squalid litter and brutal wasteful disorder.

The third necessity is *leisure*. You will understand that in using that word I imply first that all men must work for some portion of the day, and secondly that they have a positive right to claim a respite from that work: the leisure they have a right to claim, must be ample enough to allow them full rest of mind and body; a man must have time for serious individual thought, for imagination—for dreaming even—or the race of men will inevitably worsen. Even of the honourable and fitting work of which I have been speaking, which is a whole heaven asunder from the forced work of the Capitalist system, a man must not be asked to give more than his fair share; or men will become unequally developed, and there will still be a rotten place in Society.

Here then I have given you the conditions under which work worth doing, and undegrading to do, can be done: under no other conditions can it be done: if the general work of the world is not worth doing and undegrading to do it is a mockery to talk of civilization.

Well then can these conditions be obtained under the present gospel of Capital, which has for its motto "The devil take the hindmost"?

Let us look at our claim again in other words:

In a properly ordered state of Society every man willing to work should be ensured—
First—*Honourable and fitting work;*
Second—*A healthy and beautiful house;*
Third—*Full leisure for rest of mind and body.*

Now I don't suppose that anybody here will deny that it would be desirable that this claim should be satisfied: but what I want you all to think is that it is *necessary* that it be satisfied; that unless we try our utmost to satisfy it, we are but part and parcel of a society founded on robbery and injustice, condemned by the laws of the universe to destroy itself by its own efforts to exist for ever. Furthermore, I want you to think that as on the one hand it is possible to satisfy this claim, so on the other hand it is impossible to satisfy it under the present plutocratic system, which will forbid us even any serious attempt to satisfy it: the beginnings of Social Revolution must be the foundations of the re-building of the Art of the People, that is to say of the Pleasure of Life.

To say ugly words again. Do we not *know* that the greater part of men in civilized societies are dirty, ignorant, brutal—or at best, anxious about the next week's subsistence—that they are in short *poor?* And we know, when we think of it, that this is unfair.

It is an old story of men who have become rich by dishonest and tyrannical means, spending in terror of the future their ill-gotten gains liberally and in charity as 'tis called: nor are such people praised; in the old tales 'tis thought that the devil gets them after all. An old story— but I say *"De te fabula"*—of *thee* is the story told: *thou* art the man!

I say that we of the rich and well-to-do classes are daily doing it likewise: unconsciously, or half consciously it may be, we gather wealth by trading on the hard necessity of our fellows, and then we give driblets of it away to those of them who in one way or other cry out loudest to us. Our poor laws, our hospitals, our charities, organized and un-organized, are but tubs thrown to the whale; blackmail paid to lame-foot justice, that she may not hobble after us too fast.

When will the time come when honest and clear-seeing men will grow sick of all this chaos of waste, this robbing of Peter to pay Paul, which is the essence of Commercial war? When shall we band together to replace the system whose motto is "The devil take the hindmost" with a system whose motto shall be really and without qualification "One for all and all for one."

Who knows but the time may be at hand, but that we now living may see the beginning of that end which shall extinguish luxury and poverty? when the upper, middle, and lower classes shall have melted into one class, living contentedly a simple and happy life.

That is a long sentence to describe the state of things which I am asking you to help to bring about: the abolition of slavery is a shorter one and means the same thing. You may be tempted to think the end not worth striving for on one hand; or on the other to suppose, each one of you, that it is so far ahead, that nothing serious can be done towards it in our own time, and that you may as well therefore sit quiet and do nothing: let me remind you how only the other day in the lifetime of the youngest of us many thousand men of our own kindred gave their lives on the battle-field to bring to a happy ending a mere episode in the struggle for the abolition of slavery: they are blessed and happy, for the opportunity came to them, and they seized it and did their best, and the world is the wealthier for it; and if such an opportunity is offered to us shall we thrust it from us that we may sit still in ease of body, in doubt, in disease of soul? These are the days of combat: who can doubt that as he hears all round him the sounds that betoken discontent and hope and fear in high and low, the sounds of awakening courage and awakening conscience? These, I say, are the days of combat, when there is no external peace possible to an honest man; but when for that very reason the internal peace of a good conscience founded on settled convictions is the easier to win, since action for the cause is offered us.

Or, will you say that here in this quiet, constitutionally governed country of England there is no opportunity for action offered to us: if we were in gagged Germany, in gagged Austria, in Russia where a word or two might land us in Siberia or the prison or fortress of Peter and Paul—why then, indeed—

Ah! my friends, it is but a poor tribute to offer on the tombs of the martyrs of liberty, this refusal to take the torch from their dying hands! Is it not of Goethe it is told, that on hearing one say he was going to America to begin life again, he replied, "Here is America, or nowhere!" So for my part I say, "Here is Russia, or nowhere."

To say the governing classes in England are not afraid of freedom of speech, *therefore* let us abstain from speaking freely, is a strange paradox to me. Let us on the contrary press in through the breach which valiant men have made for us: if we hang back we make their labours, their sufferings, their deaths of no account.

Believe me we shall be shown that it is all or nothing: or will anyone here tell me that a Russian moujik is in a worse case than a sweating tailor's wage-slave? Do not let us deceive ourselves, the class of victims exists here as in Russia. There are fewer of them? May be—then are they of themselves more helpless, and so have more need of our help.

And how can we of the middle classes, we the capitalists and our hangers-on, help them? By renouncing our class, and on all occasions when antagonism rises up between the classes casting in our lot with the victims: with those who are condemned at the best to lack of education, refinement, leisure, pleasure and renown; and at the worst to a life lower than that of the most brutal of savages—in order that the system of competitive Commerce may endure.

There is *no* other way: and this way I tell you plainly,

will in the long run give us plentiful occasion for self-sacrifice without going to Russia. I feel sure that in this assembly there are some who are steeped in discontent with the miserable anarchy of the century of Commerce: to them I offer a means of renouncing their class by supporting a Socialist propaganda in joining the Democratic Federation, which I have the honour of representing before you, and which I believe is the only body in this country which puts forward constructive Socialism as its program.

This to my mind is opportunity enough for those of us who are discontented with the present state of things and long for an opportunity of renunciation; and it is very certain that in accepting the opportunity you will have at once to undergo some of the inconveniences of martyrdom, though without gaining its dignity at present. You will at least be mocked and laughed at by those whose mockery is a token of honour to an honest man; but you will, I don't doubt it, be looked on coldly by many excellent people, not *all* of whom will be quite stupid. You will run the risk of losing position, reputation, money, friends even: losses which are certainly pin pricks to the serious martyrdom I have spoken of; but which none the less do try the stuff a man is made of—all the more as he can escape them with little other reproach of cowardice than that which his own conscience cries out at him.

Nor can I assure you that you will for ever escape scot-free from the attacks of open tyranny. It is true that at present Capitalist Society only looks on Socialism in England with dry grins. But remember that the body of people who have for instance ruined India, starved and gagged Ireland, and tortured Egypt, have capacities in them—some ominous signs of which they have lately shown — for openly playing the tyrants' game nearer home.

So on all sides I can offer you a position which involves sacrifice; a position which will give you your "America" at home, and make you inwardly sure that you are at least of some use to the cause: and I earnestly beg you, those of you who are convinced of the justice of our cause, not

to hang back from active participation in a struggle which
—who ever helps or who ever abstains from helping—
must beyond all doubt end at last in Victory!

HOW WE LIVE AND
HOW WE MIGHT LIVE

[A lecture delivered to the Hammersmith Branch of the S.D.F. at Kelmscott House, on November 30th, 1884. First printed in *Commonweal*, 1887. *Collected Works*, XXIII, 3-26, Cole, 565-87.

Morris sees capitalist society as based on war—between nations, between rival capitalists, against colonial peoples and between classes. Only the victory of Socialist revolution can end all these wars.]

THE word Revolution, which we Socialists are so often forced to use, has a terrible sound in most people's ears, even when we have explained to them that it does not necessarily mean a change accompanied by riot and all kinds of violence, and cannot mean a change made mechanically and in the teeth of opinion by a group of men who have somehow managed to seize on the executive power for the moment. Even when we explain that we use the word revolution in its etymological sense, and mean by it a change in the basis of society, people are scared at the idea of such a vast change, and beg that you will speak of reform and not revolution. As, however, we Socialists do not at all mean by our word revolution what these worthy people mean by their word reform, I can't help thinking that it would be a mistake to use it, whatever projects we might conceal beneath its harmless envelope. So we will stick to our word, which means a change of the basis of society; it may frighten people, but it will at least warn them that there is something to be frightened about, which will be no less dangerous for being ignored; and also it may encourage some people, and will mean to them at least not a fear, but a hope.

Fear and Hope—those are the names of the two great passions which rule the race of man, and with which revolutionists have to deal; to give hope to the many oppressed and fear to the few oppressors, that is our business; if we do the first and give hope to the many, the few *must* be frightened by their hope; otherwise we do not want to frighten them; it is not revenge we want for poor people, but happiness; indeed, what revenge can be taken for all the thousands of years of the sufferings of the poor?

However, many of the oppressors of the poor, most of them, we will say, are not conscious of their being oppressors (we shall see why presently); they live in an orderly, quiet way themselves, as far as possible removed from the feelings of a Roman slave-owner or a Legree; they know that the poor exist, but their sufferings do not present themselves to them in a trenchant and dramatic way; they themselves have troubles to bear, and they think doubtless that to bear trouble is the lot of humanity; nor have they any means of comparing the troubles of their lives with those of people lower in the social scale; and if ever the thought of those heavier troubles obtrudes itself upon them, they console themselves with the maxim that people do get used to the troubles they have to bear, whatever they may be.

Indeed, as far as regards individuals at least, that is but too true, so that we have as supporters of the present state of things, however bad it may be, first those comfortable unconscious oppressors who think that they have everything to fear from any change which would involve more than the softest and most gradual of reforms, and secondly those poor people who, living hard and anxiously as they do, can hardly conceive of any change for the better happening to them, and dare not risk one tittle of their poor possessions in taking any action towards a possible bettering of their condition; so that while we can do little with the rich save inspire them with fear, it is hard indeed to give the poor any hope. It is, then, no less than reasonable that those whom we try to involve in the great struggle for a better form of life than that which we now lead should call on us to give them at least some idea of what that life may be like.

A reasonable request, but hard to satisfy, since we are living under a system that makes conscious effort towards reconstruction almost impossible: it is not unreasonable on our part to answer, "There are certain definite obstacles to the real progress of man; we can tell you what these are; take them away, and then you shall see."

However, I purpose now to offer myself as a victim for the satisfaction of those who consider that as things now go we have at least got something, and are terrified at the idea of losing their hold of that, lest they should find they are worse off than before, and have nothing. Yet in the course of my endeavour to show how we might live, I must more or less deal in negatives. I mean to say I must point out where in my opinion we fall short in our present attempt at decent life. I must ask the rich and well-to-do what sort of a position it is which they are so anxious to preserve at any cost? and if, after all, it will be such a terrible loss to them to give it up? and I must point out to the poor that they, with capacities for living a dignified and generous life, are in a position which they cannot endure without continued degradation.

How do we live, then, under our present system? Let us look at it a little.

And first, please to understand that our present system of Society is based on a state of perpetual war. Do any of you think that this is as it should be? I know that you have often been told that the competition, which is at present the rule of all production, is a good thing, and stimulates the progress of the race; but the people who tell you this should call competition by its shorter name of *war* if they wish to be honest, and you would then be free to consider whether or no war stimulates progress, otherwise than as a mad bull chasing you over your own garden may do. War, or competition, whichever you please to call it, means at the best pursuing your own advantage at the cost of some one else's loss, and in the process of it you must not be sparing of destruction even of your own possessions, or you will certainly come by the worse in the struggle. You understand that perfectly as to the kind of war in which people go out to kill and be killed; that sort of war in which ships are commissioned, for instance, "to sink, burn, and destroy"; but it appears that you are not so conscious of this waste of goods when you are only carrying on that other war called *commerce*; observe, however, that the waste is there all the same.

Now let us look at this kind of war a little closer, run through some of the forms of it, that we may see how the "burn, sink, and destroy" is carried on in it.

First, you have that form of it called national rivalry, which in good truth is nowadays the cause of all gunpowder and bayonet wars which civilized nations wage. For years past we English have been rather shy of them, except on those happy occasions when we could carry them on at no sort of risk to ourselves, when the killing was all on one side, or at all events when we hoped it would be. We have been shy of gunpowder war with a respectable enemy for a long while, and I will tell you why: It is because we have had the lion's share of the world-market; we didn't want to fight for it as a nation, for we had got it; but now this is changing in a most significant, and, to a Socialist, a most cheering way; we are losing or have lost that lion's share; it is now a desperate "competition" between the great nations of civilization for the world-market, and to-morrow it may be a desperate war for that end. As a result, the furthering of war (if it be not on too large a scale) is no longer confined to the honour-and-glory kind of old Tories, who if they meant anything at all by it meant that a Tory war would be a good occasion for damping down democracy; we have changed all that, and now it is quite another kind of politician that is wont to urge us on to "patriotism" as 'tis called. The leaders of the Progressive Liberals, as they would call themselves, long-headed persons who know well enough that social movements are going on, who are not blind to the fact that the world will move with their help or without it; these have been the Jingoes of these later days. I don't mean to say they know what they are doing: politicians, as you well know, take good care to shut their eyes to everything that may happen six months ahead; but what is being done is this: that the present system, which always must include national rivalry, is pushing us into a desperate scramble for the markets on more or less equal terms with other nations, because, once more, we have lost that command of them which we once had. Desperate is not too strong a word. We shall let this impulse to snatch markets carry us whither it will, whither it must. To-day it is successful burglary and disgrace, to-morrow it may be mere defeat and disgrace.

Now this is not a digression, although in saying this I am nearer to what is generally called politics than I shall be again. I only want to show you what commercial war comes to when it has to do with foreign nations, and that even the dullest can see how mere waste must go with it. That is how we live now with foreign nations, prepared to ruin them without war if possible, with it if necessary, let alone meantime the disgraceful exploiting of savage tribes and barbarous peoples on whom we force at once our shoddy wares and our hypocrisy at the cannon's mouth.

Well, surely Socialism can offer you something in the place of all that. It can; it can offer you peace and friendship instead of war. We might live utterly without national rivalries, acknowledging that while it is best for those who feel that they naturally form a community under one name to govern themselves, yet that no community in civilization should feel that it had interests opposed to any other, their economical condition being at any rate similar; so that any citizen of one community could fall to work and live without disturbance of his life when he was in a foreign country, and would fit into his place quite naturally; so that all civilized nations would form one great community, agreeing together as to the kind and amount of production and distribution needed; working at such and such production where it could be best produced; avoiding waste by all means. Please to think of the amount of waste which they would avoid, how much such a revolution would add to the wealth of the world! What creature on earth would be harmed by such a revolution? Nay, would not everybody be the better for it? And what hinders it? I will tell you presently.

Meantime let us pass from this "competition" between nations to that between "the organizers of labour," great firms, joint-stock companies; capitalists in short, and see how competition "stimulates production" among them: indeed it does do that; but what kind of production? Well, production of something to sell at a profit, or say production of profits: and note how war commercial stimulates that: a certain market is demanding goods; there are, say, a hundred manufacturers who make that kind of goods, and every one of them would if he could keep that market to himself, and struggles desperately to get as much of it as he can, with the obvious result that presently the thing is overdone, and the market is glutted, and all that fury of manufacture has to sink into cold ashes.

Doesn't that seem something like war to you? Can't you see the waste of it—waste of labour, skill, cunning, waste of life in short? Well you may say, but it cheapens the goods. In a sense it does; and yet only apparently, as wages have a tendency to sink for the ordinary worker in proportion as prices sink; and at what a cost do we gain this appearance of cheapness! Plainly speaking, at the cost of cheating the consumer and starving the real producer for the benefit of the gambler, who uses both consumer and producer as his milch cows. I needn't go at length into the subject of adulteration, for every one knows what kind of a part it plays in this sort of commerce; but remember that it is an absolutely necessary incident to the production of profit out of wares, which is the business of the so-salled manufacturer; and this you must understand, that, taking him in the lump, the consumer is perfectly helpless against the gambler; the goods are forced on him by their cheapness, and with them a certain kind of life which that energetic, that aggressive cheapness determines for him: for so far-reaching is this curse of commercial war that no country is safe from its ravages; the traditions of a thousand years fall before it in a month; it overruns a weak or semi-barbarous country, and whatever romance or pleasure or art existed there, is trodden down into a mire of sordidness and ugliness; the Indian or Javanese craftsman may no longer ply his craft leisurely, working a few hours a day, in producing a maze of strange beauty on a piece of cloth: a steam-engine is set a-going at Manchester, and that victory over nature and a thousand stubborn difficulties is used for the base work of producing a sort of plaster of china-clay and shoddy, and the Asiatic worker, if he is not starved to death outright, as plentifully happens, is driven himself into a factory to lower the wages of his Manchester brother worker, and nothing of character is left him except, most like, an accumulation of fear and hatred of that to him most unaccountable evil, his English master. The South Sea Islander must leave his canoe-carving, his sweet rest, and his graceful dances, and become the slave of a slave: trousers, shoddy, rum, missionary, and fatal disease—he must swallow all this civilization in the lump, and neither himself nor we can help him now till social order displaces the hideous tyranny of gambling that has ruined him.

Let those be types of the consumer: but now for the producer; I mean the real producer, the worker; how does this scramble for the plunder of the market affect him? The manufacturer, in the eagerness of his war, has had to collect into one neighbourhood a vast army of workers, he has drilled them till they are as fit as may be for his special branch of production, that is, for making a profit out of it, and with the result of their being fit for nothing else: well, when the glut comes in that market he is supplying, what happens to this army, every private in which has been depending on the steady demand in that market, and acting, as he could not choose but act, as if it were to go on for ever? You know well what happens to these men: the factory door is shut on them; on a very large part of them often, and at the best on the reserve army of labour, so busily employed in the time of inflation. What becomes of them? Nay, we know that well enough just now. But what we don't know, or don't choose to know, is that this reserve army of labour is an absolute necessity for commercial war: if *our* manufacturers had not got these poor devils whom they could draft on to their machines when the demand swelled, other manufacturers in France, or Germany, or America, would step in and take the market from them.

So you see, as we live now, it is necessary that a vast part of the industrial population should be exposed to the danger of periodical semi-starvation, and that, not for the advantage of the people in another part of the world, but for their degradation and enslavement.

Just let your minds run for a moment on the kind of waste which this means, this opening up of new markets among savage and barbarous countries which is the extreme type of the force of the profit-market on the world, and you will surely see what a hideous nightmare that profit-market is: it keeps us sweating and terrified for our livelihood, unable to read a book, or look at a picture, or have pleasant fields to walk in, or to lie in the sun, or to share in the knowledge of our time, to have in short either animal or intellectual pleasure, and for what? that we may go on living the same slavish life till we die, in order to provide for a rich man what is called a life of ease and luxury; that is to say, a life so empty, unwholesome, and degraded, that perhaps, on the whole, he is worse off than we the workers are: and as to the result of all this suffering, it is luckiest when it is nothing at all, when you can say that the wares have done nobody any good; for oftenest they have done many people harm, and we have toiled and groaned and died in making poison and destruction for our fellow-men.

Well, I say all this is war, and the result of war, the war this time, not of competing nations, but of competing firms or capitalist units: and it is this war of the firms which hinders the peace between nations which you surely have agreed with me in thinking is so necessary; for you must know that war is the very breath of the nostrils of these fighting firms, and they have now, in our times, got into their hands nearly all the political power, and they band together in each country in order to make their respective governments fulfil just two functions: the first is at home to act as a strong police force, to keep the ring in which the strong are beating down the weak; the second is to act as a piratical body-guard abroad, a petard to explode the doors which lead to the markets of the world: markets at any price abroad, uninterfered-with privilege, falsely called *laissez-faire*,[1] at any price at home, to provide these is the sole business of a government such as our industrial captains have been able to conceive of. I must now try to show you the reason of all this, and what it rests on, by trying to answer the question, Why have the profit-makers got all this power, or at least why are they able to keep it?

That takes us to the third form of war commercial: the last, and the one which all the rest is founded on. We have spoken first of the war of rival nations; next of that of rival firms: we have now to speak of rival men. As nations under the present system are driven to compete with one another for the markets of the world, and as firms or the captains of industry have to scramble for their share of the profits of the markets, so also have the workers to compete with each other—for livelihood; and it is this constant competition or war amongst them which enables the profit-grinders to make their profits, and by means of wealth so acquired to take all the executive power of the country into their hands. But here is the difference between the position of the workers and the profit-makers: to the latter, the profit-

[1] Falsely; because the privileged classes have at their back the force of the Executive by means of which to compel the unprivileged to accept the terms; if this is "free competition" there is no meaning in words.

grinders, war is necessary; you cannot have profit-making without competition, individual, corporate, and national; but you may work for a livelihood without competing; you may combine instead of competing.

I have said war was the life-breath of the profit-makers; in like manner, combination is the life of the workers. The working classes or proletariat cannot even exist as a class without combination of some sort. The necessity which forced the profit-grinders to collect their men first into workshops working by the division of labour, and next into great factories worked by machinery, and so gradually draw them into the great towns and centres of civilization, gave birth to a distinct working class or proletariat: and this it was which gave them their *mechanical* existence, so to say. But note, that they are indeed combined into social groups for the production of wares, but only as yet mechanically; they do not know what they are working at, nor whom they are working for, because they are combining to produce wares of which the profit of a master forms an essential part, instead of goods for their own use: as long as they do this, and compete with each other for leave to do it, they will be, and will feel themselves to be, simply a part of those competing firms I have been speaking of; they will be in fact just a part of the machinery for the production of profit; and so long as this lasts it will be the aim of the masters or profit-makers to decrease the market value of this human part of the machinery; that is to say, since they already hold in their hands the labour of dead men in the form of capital and machinery, it is their interest, or we will say their necessity, to pay as little as they can help for the labour of living men which they have to buy from day to day: and since the workmen they employ have nothing but their labour-power, they are compelled to underbid one another for employment and wages, and so enable the capitalist to play his game.

I have said that, as things go, the workers are a part of the competing firms, an adjunct of capital. Nevertheless, they are only so by compulsion; and, even without their being conscious of it, they struggle against that compulsion and its immediate results, the lowering of their wages, of their standard of life: and this they do, and must do, both as a class and individually: just as the slave of the great Roman lord, though he distinctly felt himself to be a part of the household, yet collectively was a force in reserve for its destruction, and individually stole from his lord whenever he could safely do so. So here, you see, is another form of war necessary to the way we live now, the war of class against class, which, when it rises to its height, and it seems to be rising at present, will destroy those other forms of war we have been speaking of; will make the position of the profit-makers, of perpetual commercial war, untenable; will destroy the present system of competitive privilege, or commercial war.

Now observe, I said that to the existence of the workers it was combination, not competition, that was necessary, while to that of the profit-makers combination was impossible, and war necessary. The present position of the workers is that of the machinery of commerce, or in plainer words its slaves; when they change that position and become free, the class of profit-makers must cease to exist; and what will then be the position of the workers? Even as it is they are the one necessary part of society, the life-giving part; the other classes are but hangers-on who live on them. But what should they be, what will they be, when they, once for all, come to know their real power, and cease competing with one another for livelihood? I will tell you: they will be society, they will be the community. And being society—that is, there being no class outside them to contend with—they can then regulate their labour in accordance with their own real needs.

There is much talk about supply and demand, but the supply and demand usually meant is an artificial one; it is under the sway of the gambling market; the demand is forced, as I hinted above, before it is supplied; nor, as each producer is working against all the rest, can the producers hold their hands, till the market is glutted and the workers, thrown out on the streets, hear that there has been over-production, amidst which over-plus of unsaleable goods they go ill supplied with even necessaries, because the wealth which they themselves have created is "ill distributed," as we call it—that is, unjustly taken away from them.

When the workers are society they will regulate their labour, so that the supply and demand shall be genuine, not gambling; the two will then be commensurate, for it is the same society which demands that also supplies; there will be no more artificial famines then, no more poverty amidst over-production, amidst too great a stock of the very things which should supply poverty and turn it into well-being. In short, there will be no waste and therefore no tyranny.

Well, now, what Socialism offers you in place of these artificial famines, with their so-called over-production, is, once more, regulation of the markets; supply and demand commensurate; no gambling, and consequently (once more) no waste; not overwork and weariness for the worker one month, and the next no work and terror of starvation, but steady work and plenty of leisure every month; not cheap market wares, that is to say, adulterated wares, with scarcely any *good* in them, mere scaffold-poles for building up profits; no labour would be spent on such things as these, which people would cease to want when they ceased to be slaves. Not these, but such goods as best fulfilled the real uses of the consumers would labour be set to make; for, profit being abolished, people could have what they wanted instead of what the profit-grinders at home and abroad forced them to take.

For what I want you to understand is this: that in every civilized country at least there is plenty for all—is, or at any rate might be. Even with labour so misdirected as it is at present, an equitable distribution of the wealth we have would make all people comparatively comfortable; but that is nothing to the wealth we might have if labour were not misdirected.

Observe, in the early days of the history of man he was the slave of his most immediate necessities; Nature was mighty and he was feeble, and he had to wage constant war with her for his daily food and such shelter as he could get. His life was bound down and limited by this constant struggle; all his morals, laws, religion, are in fact the outcome and the reflection of this ceaseless toil of earning his livelihood. Time passed, and little by little, step by step, he grew stronger, till now after all these ages he has almost completely conquered Nature, and one would think should now have leisure to turn his thoughts towards higher things than procuring to-morrow's dinner. But, alas! his progress has been broken and halting; and though he has indeed conquered Nature and has her forces under his control to do what he will with, he still has himself to conquer, he still has to think how he will best use those forces which he has mastered. At present he uses them blindly, foolishly, as one driven by mere fate. It would almost seem as if some phantom of the ceaseless pursuit of food which was once the master of the savage was still haunting the civilized man; who toils in a dream, as it were, haunted by mere dim unreal hopes, born of vague recollections of the days gone by. Out of that dream he must wake, and face things as they really are. The conquest of Nature is complete, may we not say? and now our business is and has for long been the organization of man, who wields the forces of Nature. Nor till this is attempted at least shall we ever be free of that terrible phantom of fear of starvation which, with its brother devil, desire of domination, drives us into injustice, cruelty, and dastardliness of all kinds: to cease to fear our fellows and learn to depend on them, to do away with competition and build up co-operation, is our one necessity.

Now, to get closer to details; you probably know that every man in civilization is worth, so to say, more than his skin; working, as he must work, socially, he can produce more than will keep himself alive and in fair condition; and this has been so for many centuries, from the time, in fact, when warring tribes began to make their conquered enemies slaves instead of killing them; and of course his capacity of producing these extras has gone on increasing faster and faster, till to-day one man will weave, for instance, as much cloth in a week as will clothe a whole village for years; and the real question of civilization has always been what are we to do with extra produce of labour—a question which the phantom, fear of starvation, and its fellow, desire of domination, has driven men to answer pretty badly always, and worst of all perhaps in these present days, when the extra produce has grown with such prodigious speed. The practical answer has always been for man to struggle with his fellow for private possession of undue shares of these extras, and all kinds of devices have been employed by those who found themselves in possession of the power of taking them from others to keep those whom they had robbed in perpetual subjection; and these latter, as I have already hinted, had no chance of resisting this fleecing as long as they were few and scattered, and consequently could have little sense of their common oppression. But now that, owing to the very pursuit of these undue shares of profit, or extra earnings, men have become more dependent on each other for production, and have been driven, as I said before, to combine together for that end more completely, the power of the workers—that is to say, of the robbed or fleeced class—has enormously increased, and it only remains for them to understand that they have this power. When they do that they will be able to give the right answer to the question what is to be done with the extra products of labour over and above what will keep the labourer alive to labour: which answer is, that the worker will have all that he produces, and not be fleeced at all: and remember that he produces collectively, and therefore he will do effectively what work is required of him according to his capacity, and of the produce of that work he will have what he needs; because, you see, he cannot *use* more than he needs—he can only *waste* it.

If this arrangement seems to you preposterously ideal, as it well may, looking at our present condition, I must back it up by saying that when men are organized so that their labour is not wasted, they will be relieved from the fear of starvation and the desire of domination, and will have freedom and leisure to look round and see what they really do need.

Now something of that I can conceive for my own self, and I will lay my ideas before you, so that you may compare them with your own, asking you always to remember that the very differences in men's capacities and desires, after the common need of food and shelter is satisfied, will make it easier to deal with their desires in a communal state of things.

What is it that I need, therefore, which my surrounding circumstances can give me—my dealings with my fellow-men—setting aside inevitable accidents which co-operation and forethought cannot control, if there be such?

Well, first of all I claim good health; and I say that a vast proportion of people in civilization scarcely even know what that means. To feel mere life a pleasure; to enjoy the moving one's limbs and exercising one's bodily powers; to play, as it were, with sun and wind and rain; to rejoice in satisfying the due bodily appetites of a human animal without fear of degradation or sense of wrongdoing; yes, and therewithal to be well-formed, straight-limbed, strongly knit, expressive of countenance—to be, in a word, beautiful—that also I claim. If we cannot have this claim satisfied, we are but poor creatures after all; and I claim it in the teeth of those terrible doctrines of asceticism, which, born of the despair of the oppressed and degraded, have been for so many ages used as instruments for the continuance of that oppression and degradation.

And I believe that this claim for a healthy body for all of us carries with it all other due claims: for who knows where the seeds of disease which even rich people suffer from were first sown: from the luxury of an ancestor, perhaps; yet often, I suspect, from his poverty. And for the poor: a distinguished physicist has said that the poor suffer always from one disease—hunger; and at least I know this, that if a man is overworked in any degree he cannot enjoy the sort of health I am speaking of; nor can he if he is continually chained to one dull round of mechanical work, with no hope at the other end of it; nor if he lives in continual sordid anxiety for his livelihood, nor if he is ill housed, nor if he is deprived of all enjoyment of the natural beauty of the world, nor if he has no amusement to quicken the flow of his spirits from time to time: all these things, which touch more or less directly on his bodily condition, are born of the claim I make to live in good health; indeed, I suspect that these good conditions must have been in force for several generations before a population in general will be really healthy, as I have hinted above; but also I doubt not that in the course of time they would, joined to other conditions, of which more hereafter, gradually breed such a population, living in enjoyment of animal life at least, happy therefore, and beautiful according to the beauty of their race. On this point I may note that the very variations in the races of men are caused by the conditions under which they live, and though in these rougher parts of the world we lack some of the advantages of climate and surroundings, yet, if we were working for livelihood and not for profit, we might easily neutralize many of the disadvantages of our climate, at least enough to give due scope to the full development of our race.

Now the next thing I claim is education. And you must not say that every English child is educated now; that sort of education will not answer my claim, though I cheerfully admit it is something: something, and yet after all only class education. What I claim is liberal education; opportunity, that is, to have my share of whatever knowledge there is in the world according to my capacity or bent of mind, historical or scientific; and also to have my share of skill of hand which is about in the world, either in the industrial handicrafts or in the fine arts; picture-painting, sculpture, music, acting, or the like: I claim to be taught, if I can be taught, more than one craft to exercise for the benefit of the community. You may think this a large claim, but I am clear it is not too large a claim if the community is to have any gain out of my special capacities, if we are not all to be beaten down to a dull level of mediocrity as we are now, all but the very strongest and toughest of us.

But also I know that this claim for education involves one for public advantages in the shape of public libraries, schools, and the like, such as no private person, not even the richest, could command: but these I claim very confidently, being sure that no reasonable community could bear to be without such help to a decent life.

Again, the claim for education involves a claim for abundant leisure, which once more I make with confidence; because when once we have shaken off the slavery of profit, labour would be organized so unwastefully that no heavy burden would be laid on the individual citizens; every one of whom as a matter of course would have to pay his toll of some obviously useful work. At present you must note that all the amazing machinery which we have invented has served only to increase the amount of profit-bearing wares; in other words, to increase the amount of profit pouched by individuals for their own advantage, part of which profit they use as capital for the production of more profit, with ever the same waste attached to it; and part as private riches or means for luxurious living, which again is sheer waste—is in fact to be looked on as a kind of bonfire in which rich men burn up the product of the labour they have fleeced from the workers beyond what they themselves can use. So I say that, in spite of our inventions, no worker works under the present system an hour the less on account of those labour-saving machines, so called. But under a happier state of things they would be used simply for saving labour, with the result of a vast amount of leisure gained for the community to be added to that gained by the avoidance of the waste of useless luxury, and the abolition of the service of commercial war.

And I may say that as to that leisure, as I should in no

case do any harm to any one with it, so I should often do some direct good to the community with it, by practising arts or occupations for my hands or brain which would give pleasure to many of the citizens; in other words, a great deal of the best work done would be done in the leisure time of men relieved from any anxiety as to their livelihood, and eager to exercise their special talent, as all men, nay, all animals are.

Now, again this leisure would enable me to please myself and expand my mind by travelling if I had a mind to it; because, say, for instance, that I were a shoemaker; if due social order were established, it by no means follows that I should always be obliged to make shoes in one place; a due amount of easily conceivable arrangement would enable me to make shoes in Rome, say, for three months, and to come back with new ideas of building, gathered from the sight of the works of past ages, amongst other things which would perhaps be of service in London.

But now, in order that my leisure might not degenerate into idleness and aimlessness, I must set up a claim for due work to do. Nothing to my mind is more important than this demand, and I must ask your leave to say something about it. I have mentioned that I should probably use my leisure for doing a good deal of what is now called work; but it is clear that if I am a member of a Socialist Community I must do my due share of rougher work than this—my due share of what my capacity enables me to do, that is; no fitting of me to a Procrustean bed; but even that share of work necessary to the existence of the simplest social life must, in the first place, whatever else it is, be reasonable work; that is, it must be such work as a good citizen can see the necessity for; as a member of the community, I must have agreed to do it.

To take two strong instances of the contrary, I won't submit to be dressed up in red and marched off to shoot at my French or German or Arab friend in a quarrel that I don't understand; I will rebel sooner than do that.

Nor will I submit to waste my time and energies in

making some trifling toy which I know only a fool can desire; I will rebel sooner than do that.

However, you may be sure that in a state of social order I shall have no need to rebel against any such pieces of unreason; only I am forced to speak from the way we live to the way we might live.

Again, if the necessary reasonable work be of a mechanical kind, I must be helped to do it by a machine, not to cheapen my labour, but so that as little time as possible may be spent upon it, and that I may be able to think of other things while I am tending the machine. And if the work be specially rough or exhausting, you will, I am sure, agree with me in saying that I must take turns in doing it with other people; I mean I mustn't, for instance, be expected to spend my working hours always at the bottom of a coal-pit. I think such work as that ought to be largely volunteer work, and done, as I say, in spells. And what I say of very rough work I say also of nasty work. On the other hand, I should think very little of the manhood of a stout and healthy man who did not feel a pleasure in doing rough work; always supposing him to work under the conditions I have been speaking of—namely, feeling that it was useful (and consequently honoured), and that it was not continuous or hopeless, and that he was really doing it of his own free will.

The last claim I make for my work is that the places I worked in, factories or workshops, should be pleasant, just as the fields where our most necessary work is done are pleasant. Believe me there is nothing in the world to prevent this being done, save the necessity of making profits on all wares; in other words, the wares are cheapened at the expense of people being forced to work in crowded, unwholesome, squalid, noisy dens: that is to say, they are cheapened at the expense of the workman's life.

Well, so much for my claims as to my *necessary* work, my tribute to the community. I believe people would find, as they advanced in their capacity for carrying on social order, that life so lived was much less expensive than we now can have any idea of, and that, after a little, people would rather be anxious to seek work than to avoid it; that our working hours would rather be merry parties of men and maids, young men and old enjoying themselves over their work, than the grumpy weariness it mostly is now. Then would come the time for the new birth of art, so much talked of, so long deferred; people could not help showing their mirth and pleasure in their work, and would be always wishing to express it in a tangible and more or less enduring form, and the workshop would once more be a school of art, whose influence no one could escape from.

And, again, that word art leads me to my last claim, which is that the material surroundings of my life should be pleasant, generous, and beautiful; that I know is a large claim, but this I will say about it, that if it cannot be satisfied, if every civilized community cannot provide such surroundings for all its members, I do not want the world to go on; it is a mere misery that man has ever existed. I do not think it possible under the present circumstances to speak too strongly on this point. I feel sure that the time will come when people will find it difficult to believe that a rich community such as ours, having such command over external Nature, could have submitted to live such a mean, shabby, dirty life as we do.

And once for all, there is nothing in our circumstances save the hunting of profit that drives us into it. It is profit which draws men into enormous unmanageable aggregations called towns, for instance; profit which crowds them up when they are there into quarters without gardens or open spaces; profit which won't take the most ordinary precautions against wrapping a whole district in a cloud of sulphurous smoke; which turns beautiful rivers into filthy sewers, which condemns all but the rich to live in houses idiotically cramped and confined at the best, and at the worst in houses for whose wretchedness there is no name.

I say it is almost incredible that we should bear such

crass stupidity as this; nor should we if we could help it. We shall not bear it when the workers get out of their heads that they are but an appendage to profit-grinding, that the more profits that are made the more employment at high wages there will be for them, and that therefore all the incredible filth, disorder, and degradation of modern civilization are signs of their prosperity. So far from that, they are signs of their slavery. When they are no longer slaves they will claim as a matter of course that every man and every family should be generously lodged; that every child should be able to play in a garden close to the place his parents live in; that the houses should by their obvious decency and order be ornaments to Nature, not disfigurements of it; for the decency and order above mentioned when carried to the due pitch would most assuredly lead to beauty in building. All this, of course, would mean the people—that is, all society—duly organized, having in its own hands the means of production, to be *owned* by no individual, but used by all as occasion called for its use, and can only be done on those terms; on any other terms people will be driven to accumulate private wealth for themselves, and thus, as we have seen, to waste the goods of the community and perpetuate the division into classes, which means continual war and waste.

As to what extent it may be necessary or desirable for people under social order to live in common, we may differ pretty much according to our tendencies towards social life. For my part I can't see why we should think it a hardship to eat with the people we work with; I am sure that as to many things, such as valuable books, pictures, and splendour of surroundings, we shall find it better to club our means together; and I must say that often when I have been sickened by the stupidity of the mean idiotic rabbit warrens that rich men build for themselves in Bayswater and elsewhere, I console myself with visions of the noble communal hall of the future, unsparing of materials, generous in worthy ornament, alive with the noblest thoughts of our time, and the past, embodied in the best art which a free and manly people could produce; such an abode of man as no private enterprise could come anywhere near for beauty and fitness, because only collective thought and collective life could cherish the aspirations which would give birth to its beauty, or have the skill and leisure to carry them out. I for my part should think it much the reverse of a hardship if I had to read my books and meet my friends in such a place; nor do I think I am better off to live in a vulgar stuccoed house crowded with upholstery that I despise, in all respects degrading to the mind and enervating to the body to live in, simply because I call it my own, or my house.

It is not an original remark, but I make it here, that my home is where I meet people with whom I sympathize, whom I love.

Well, that is my opinion as a middle-class man. Whether a working-class man would think his family possession of his wretched little room better than his share of the palace of which I have spoken, I must leave to his opinion, and to the imagination of the middle class, who perhaps may sometimes conceive the fact that the said worker is cramped for space and comfort—say on washing-day.

Before I leave this matter of the surroundings of life, I wish to meet a possible objection. I have spoken of machinery being used freely for releasing people from the more mechanical and repulsive part of necessary labour; and I know that to some cultivated people, people of the artistic turn of mind, machinery is particularly distasteful, and they will be apt to say you will never get your surroundings pleasant so long as you are surrounded by machinery. I don't quite admit that; it is the allowing machines to be our masters and not our servants that so injures the beauty of life nowadays. In other words, it is the token of the terrible crime we have fallen into of using our control of the powers of Nature for the purpose of enslaving people, we care less meantime of how much happiness we rob their lives of.

Yet for the consolation of the artists I will say that I believe indeed that a state of social order would probably lead at first to a great development of machinery for really useful purposes, because people will still be anxious about getting through the work necessary to holding society together; but that after a while they will find that there is not so much work to do as they expected, and that then they will have leisure to reconsider the whole subject; and if it seems to them that a certain industry would be carried on more pleasantly as regards the worker, and more effectually as regards the goods, by using hand-work rather than machinery, they will certainly get rid of their machinery, because it will be possible for them to do so. It isn't possible now; we are not at liberty to do so; we are slaves to the monsters which we have created. And I have a kind of hope that the very elaboration of machinery in a society whose purpose is not the multiplication of labour, as it now is, but the carrying on of a pleasant life, as it would be under social order—that the elaboration of machinery, I say, will lead to the simplification of life, and so once more to the limitation of machinery.

Well, I will now let my claims for decent life stand as I have made them. To sum them up in brief, they are: First, a healthy body; second, an active mind in sympathy with the past, the present, and the future; thirdly, occupation fit for a healthy body and an active mind; and fourthly, a beautiful world to live in.

These are the conditions of life which the refined man of all ages has set before him as the thing above all others to be attained. Too often he has been so foiled in their pursuit that he has turned longing eyes backward to the days before civilization, when man's sole business was getting himself food from day to day, and hope was dormant in him, or at least could not be expressed by him.

Indeed, if civilization (as many think) forbids the realization of the hope to attain such conditions of life, then civilization forbids mankind to be happy; and if that be the case, then let us stifle all aspirations towards progress

—nay, all feelings of mutual good-will and affection between men—and snatch each one of us what we can from the heap of wealth that fools create for rogues to grow fat on; or better still, let us as speedily as possible find some means of dying like men, since we are forbidden to live like men.

Rather, however, take courage, and believe that we of this age, in spite of all its torment and disorder, have been born to a wonderful heritage fashioned of the work of those that have gone before us; and that the day of the organization of man is dawning. It is not we who can build up the new social order; the past ages have done the most of that work for us; but we can clear our eyes to the signs of the times, and we shall then see that the attainment of a good condition of life is being made possible for us, and that it is now our business to stretch out our hands, to take it.

And how? Chiefly, I think, by educating people to a sense of their capacities as men, so that they may be able to use to their own good the political power which is rapidly being thrust upon them; to get them to see that the old system of organizing labour for *individual profit* is becoming unmanageable, and that the whole people have now got to choose between the confusion resulting from the break up of that system and the determination to take in hand the labour now organized for profit, and use its organization for the livelihood of the community: to get people to see that individual profit-makers are not a necessity for labour but an obstruction to it, and that not only or chiefly because they are the perpetual pensioners of labour, as they are, but rather because of the waste which their existence as a class necessitates. All this we have to teach people, when we have taught ourselves; and I admit that the work is long and burdensome; as I began by saying, people have been made so timorous of change by the terror of starvation that even the unluckiest of them are stolid and hard to move. Hard as the work is, however, its reward is not doubtful. The mere fact that a body of men, however small, are banded together as Socialist missionaries shows that the change is going on. As the working classes, the real organic part of society, take in these ideas, hope will arise in them, and they will claim changes in society, many of which doubtless will not tend directly towards their emancipation, because they will be claimed without due knowledge of the one thing necessary to claim, *equality of condition;* but which indirectly will help to break up our rotten sham society, while that claim for equality of condition will be made constantly and with growing loudness till it *must* be listened to, and then at last it will only be a step over the border, and the civilized world will be socialized; and, looking back on what has been, we shall be astonished to think of how long we submitted to live as we live now.

THE HOPES OF CIVILIZATION

[A lecture delivered before the Hammersmith Branch of the Socialist League, on June 14th, 1885. First published in *Signs of Change*, 1888, *Collected Works*, XXIII,59-80, Jackson, 279-97.

I have included this lecture as an excellent example of Morris' historical method of explaining the class struggle. It ends with a striking tribute to the work of Marx whose influence it shows throughout.]

EVERY age has had its hopes, hopes that look to something beyond the life of the age itself, hopes that try to pierce into the future; and, strange to say, I believe that those hopes have been stronger not in the heyday of the epoch which has given them birth, but rather in its decadence and times of corruption: in sober truth it may well be that these hopes are but a reflection in those that live happily and comfortably of the vain longings of those others who suffer with little power of expressing their sufferings in an audible voice: when all goes well the happy world forgets these people and their desires, sure as it is that their woes are not dangerous to them the wealthy: whereas when the woes and grief of the poor begin to rise to a point beyond the endurance of men, fear conscious or unconscious falls upon the rich, and they begin to look about them to see what there may be among the elements of their society which may be used as palliatives for the misery which, long existing and ever growing greater among the slaves of that society, is now at last forcing itself on the attention of the masters. Times of change, disruption, and revolution are naturally times of hope also, and not seldom the hopes of something better to come are the first tokens that tell people that revolution is at hand, though commonly such tokens are no more believed than Cassandra's prophecies, or are even taken in a contrary sense by those who have anything to lose; since they look upon them as signs of the prosperity of the times, and the long endurance of that state of things which is so kind to them. Let us then see what the hopes of civilization are like to-day: for indeed I purpose speaking of our own times chiefly, and will leave for the present all mention of that older civilization which was destroyed by the healthy barbarism out of which our present society has grown.

Yet a few words may be necessary concerning the birth of our present epoch and the hopes it gave rise to, and what has become of them: that will not take us very far back in history; as to my mind our modern civilization begins with the stirring period about the time of the Reformation in England, the time which in the then more important countries of the Continent is known as the period of the Renaissance, the so-called new birth of art and learning.

And first remember that this period includes the death-throes of feudalism, with all the good and evil which that system bore with it. For centuries past its end was getting ready by the gradual weakening of the bonds of the great hierarchy which held men together: the characteristics of those bonds were, theoretically at least, personal rights and personal duties between superior and inferior all down the scale; each man was born, so to say, subject to these conditions, and the mere accidents of his life could not free him from them: commerce, in our sense of the word, there was none; capitalistic manufacture, capitalistic exchange was unknown: to buy goods cheap that you might sell them dear was a legal offence (forestalling): to buy goods in the market in the morning and to sell them in the afternoon in the same place was not thought a useful occupation and was forbidden under the name of regrating; usury, instead of leading as now directly to the highest offices of the State, was thought wrong, and the profit of it mostly fell to the chosen people of God: the robbery of the workers, thought necessary then as now to the very existence of the State, was carried out quite crudely without any concealment or excuse by arbitrary taxation or open violence: on the other hand, life was easy, and common necessaries plenteous; the holidays of the Church were holidays in the modern sense of the word, downright play-days, and there were ninety-six obligatory ones: nor were the people tame and sheep-like, but as rough-handed and bold a set of good fellows as ever rubbed through life under the sun.

I remember three passages, from contemporary history or gossip, about the life of those times which luck has left us, and which illustrate curiously the change that has taken place in the habits of Englishmen. A lady writing from Norfolk 400 years ago to her husband in London, amidst various commissions for tapestries, groceries, and gowns, bids him also not to forget to bring back with him a good supply of cross-bows and bolts, since the windows of their hall were too low to be handy for long-bow shooting. A German traveller, writing quite at the end of the mediaeval period, speaks of the English as the laziest and proudest people and the best cooks in Europe. A Spanish ambassador about the same period says, "These English live in houses built of sticks and mud,[1] but therein they fare as plenteously as lords."

Indeed, I confess that it is with a strange emotion that I recall these times and try to realize the life of our fore-fathers, men who were named like ourselves, spoke nearly the same tongue, lived on the same spots of earth, and therewithal were as different from us in manners, habits, ways of life and thought, as though they lived on another planet. The very face of the country has changed; not merely I mean in London and the great manufacturing centres, but through the country generally; there is no piece

---

[1] I suppose he was speaking of the frame houses of Kent.

of English ground, except such places as Salisbury Plain, but bears witness to the amazing change which 400 years has brought upon us.

Not seldom I please myself with trying to realize the face of mediaeval England: the many chases and great woods, the stretches of common tillage and common pasture quite unenclosed; the rough husbandry of the tilled parts, the unimproved breeds of cattle, sheep, and swine; especially the latter, so lank and long and lathy, looking so strange to us; the strings of packhorses along the bridle-roads, the scantiness of the wheel-roads, scarce any except those left by the Romans, and those made from monastery to monastery: the scarcity of bridges, and people using ferries instead, or fords where they could; the little towns, well bechurched, often walled: the villages just where they are now (except for those that have nothing but the church left to tell of them), but better and more populous; their churches, some big and handsome, some small and curious, but all crowded with altars and furniture and gay with pictures and ornament; the many religious houses, with their glorious architecture; the beautiful manor-houses, some of them castles once, and survivals from an earlier period; some new and elegant; some out of all proportion small for the importance of their lords. How strange it would be to us if we could be landed in fourteenth-century England! Unless we saw the crest of some familiar hill, like that which yet bears upon it a symbol of an English tribe, and from which, looking down on the plain where Alfred was born, I once had many such ponderings, we should not know into what country of the world we were come: the name is left, scarce a thing else.

And when I think of this it quickens my hope of what may be: even so it will be with us in time to come; all will have changed, and another people will be dwelling here in England, who, although they may be of our blood and bear our name, will wonder how we lived in the nineteenth century.

Well, under all that rigidly ordered caste society of the

fourteenth century, with its rough plenty, its sauntering life, its cool acceptance of rudeness and violence, there was going on a keen struggle of classes which carried with it the hope of progress of those days: the serfs gradually getting freed, and becoming some of them the town population, the first journeymen, or "free-labourers," so called, some of them the copyholders of agricultural land: the corporations of the towns gathered power; the craft-gilds grew into perfection and corruption, the power of the Crown increased, attended with nascent bureaucracy; in short, the middle class was forming underneath the outward show of feudalism still intact: and all was getting ready for the beginning of the great commercial epoch in whose *latter* days I would fain hope we are living. That epoch began with the portentous change of agriculture which means cultivating for profit instead of for livelihood, and which carried with it the expropriation of the *people* from the land, the extinction of the yeoman, and the rise of the capitalist farmer; and the growth of the town population, which, swelled by the drift of the landless vagabonds and masterless men, grew into a definite proletariat or class of free-workmen; and their existence made that of the embryo capitalist-manufacturer also possible; and the reign of commercial contract and cash payment began to take the place of the old feudal hierarchy, with its many-linked chain of personal responsibilities. The latter half of the seventeenth century, the reign of Charles II, saw the last blow struck at this feudal system, when the landowners' military service was abolished, and they became simple owners of property that had no duties attached to it save the payment of a land-tax.

The hopes of the early part of the commercial period may be read in almost every book of the time, expressed in various degrees of dull or amusing pedantry, and show a naif arrogance and contempt of the times just past through which nothing but the utmost simplicity of ignorance could have attained to. But the times were stirring, and gave birth to the most powerful individualities in many branches of literature, and More and Campanella, at least from the midst of the exuberant triumph of young commercialism, gave to the world prophetic hopes of times yet to come when that commercialism itself should have given place to the society which we hope will be the next transform of civilization into something else: into a new social life.

This period of early and exuberant hope passed into the next stage of sober realization of many of them, for commerce grew and grew, and moulded all society to its needs: the workman of the sixteenth century worked still as an individual with little co-operation, and scarce any division of labour: by the end of the seventeenth he had become only a part of a group which by that time was in the handicrafts the real unit of production; division of labour even at that period had quite destroyed his individuality, and the worker was but part of a machine; all through the eighteenth century this system went on progressing towards perfection, till to most men at that period, to most of those who were in any way capable of expressing their thoughts, civilization had already reached a high stage of perfection, and was certain to go on from better to better.

These hopes were not on the surface of a very revolutionary kind, but nevertheless the class struggle still went on, and quite openly too; for the remains of feudality, aided by the mere mask and grimace of the religion which was once a real part of the feudal system, hampered the progress of commerce sorely, and seemed a thousandfold more powerful than it really was; because in spite of the class struggle there was really a covert alliance between the powerful middle classes who were the children of commerce and their old masters the aristocracy; an unconscious understanding between them rather, in the midst of their contest, that certain matters were to be respected even by the advanced party. The contest and civil war between the king and the commons in England in the seventeenth century illustrate this well: the caution with which privilege was attacked in the beginning of the struggle, the unwillingness of all the leaders save a few enthusiasts to carry matters to their logical consequences, even when the march of events had developed the antagonism between aristocratic privilege and middle-class freedom of contract (so called); finally, the crystallization of the new order conquered by the sword of Naseby into a mongrel condition of things between privilege and bourgeois freedom, the defeat and grief of the purist Republicans, and the horror at and swift extinction of the Levellers, the pioneers of Socialism in that day, all point to the fact that the "party of progress," as we should call it now, was determined after all that privilege should not be abolished further than its own standpoint.

The seventeenth century ended in the great Whig revolution in England, and, as I said, commerce throve and grew enormously, and the power of the middle classes increased proportionately and all things seemed going smoothly with them till, at last in France, the culminating corruption of a society still nominally existing for the benefit of the privileged aristocracy, forced their hand: the old order of things, backed as it was by the power of the executive, by that semblance of overwhelming physical force which is the real and only cement of a society founded on the slavery of the many—the aristocratic power—seemed strong and almost inexpugnable: and since any stick will do to beat a dog with, the middle classes in France were forced to take up the first stick that lay ready to hand if they were not to give way to the aristocrats, which indeed the whole evolution of history forbade them to do. Therefore, as in England in the seventeenth century, the middle classes allied themselves to religious and republican, and even communistic enthusiasts, with the intention, firm though unexpressed, to keep them down when they had mounted to power by their means, so in France they had to ally themselves with the proletariat; which, shamefully oppressed and degraded as it had been, now for the first time in history began to feel its power, the power of numbers: by means of this help they triumphed over aristocratic privilege, but, on the other hand, although the proletariat was speedily reduced again to a position not much better than that it had held before the revolution, the part it played therein gave a new and terrible character to that revolution, and from that time forward the class struggle entered on to a new phase; the middle classes had gained a complete victory, which in France carried with it all the outward signs of victory, though in England they chose to consider a certain part of themselves an aristocracy, who had indeed little signs of aristocracy about them either for good or for evil, being in very few cases of long descent, and being in their manners and ideas unmistakably *bourgeois*.

So was accomplished the second act of the great class struggle with whose first act began the age of commerce; as to the hopes of this period of the revolution we all know how extravagant they were; what a complete regeneration of the world was expected to result from the abolition of the grossest form of privilege; and I must say that, before we mock at the extravagance of those hopes, we should try to put ourselves in the place of those that held them, and try to conceive how the privilege of the old noblesse must have galled the respectable well-to-do people of that time. Well, the reasonable part of those hopes were realized by the revolution; in other words, it accomplished what it really aimed at, the freeing of commerce from the fetters of sham feudality; or, in other words, the destruction of aristocratic privilege. The more extravagant part of the hopes expressed by the eighteenth-century revolution were vague enough, and tended in the direction of supposing that the working classes would be benefited by what was to the interest of the middle class in some way quite unexplained—by a kind of magic, one may say—which welfare of the workers, as it was never directly aimed at, but only hoped for by the way, so also did not come about by any such magical means, and the triumphant middle classes began gradually to find themselves looked upon no longer as rebellious servants, but as oppressive masters.

The middle class had freed commerce from her fetters of privilege, and had freed thought from her fetters of theology, at least partially; but it had not freed, nor attempted to free, labour from its fetters. The leaders of the French Revolution, even amidst the fears, suspicions, and slaughter of the Terror, upheld the rights of "property" so called, though a new pioneer or prophet appeared in France, analogous in some respects to the Levellers of Cromwell's time, but, as might be expected, far more advanced and reasonable than they were. Gracchus Babeuf and his fellows were treated as criminals, and died or suffered the torture of prison for attempting to put into practice those words which the Republic still carried on its banners, and Liberty, Fraternity, and Equality were interpreted in a middle-class, or if you please a Jesuitical sense, as the rewards of success for those who could struggle into an exclusive class; and at last property had to be defended by a military adventurer, and the Revolution seemed to have ended with Napoleonism.

Nevertheless, the Revolution was not dead, nor was it possible to say thus far and no farther to the rising tide. Commerce, which had created the propertyless proletariat throughout civilization, had still another part to play, which is not yet played out; she had and has to teach the workers to know what they are; to educate them, to consolidate them, and not only to give them aspirations for their advancement as a class, but to make means for them to realize those aspirations. All this she did, nor loitered in her work either; from the beginning of the nineteenth century the history of civilization is really the history of the last of the class struggles which was inaugurated by the French Revolution; and England, who all through the times of the Revolution and the Cæsarism which followed it appeared to be the steady foe of Revolution, was really as steadily furthering it; her natural conditions, her store of coal and minerals, her temperate climate, extensive sea-board and many harbours, and lastly her position as the outpost of Europe looking into America across the ocean, doomed her to be for a time at least the mistress of the commerce of the civilized world, and its agent with barbarous and semi-barbarous countries. The necessities of this destiny drove her into the implacable war with France, a war which, nominally waged on behalf of monarchical principles, was really, though doubtless unconsciously, carried on for the possession of the foreign and colonial markets. She came out victorious from that war, and fully prepared to take advantage of the industrial revolution which had been going on the while, and which I now ask you to note.

I have said that the eighteenth century perfected the system of labour which took the place of the mediæval system, under which a workman individually carried his piece of work all through its various stages from the first to the last.

This new system, the first change in industrial production since the Middle Ages, is known as the system of division of labour, wherein, as I said, the unit of labour is a group, not a man; the individual workman in this system is kept life-long at the performance of some task quite petty in itself, and which he soon masters, and having mastered it has nothing more to do but to go on increasing his speed of hand under the spur of competition with his fellows, until he has become the perfect machine which it is his ultimate duty to become, since without attaining to that end he must die or become a pauper. You can well imagine how this glorious invention of division of labour, this complete destruction of individuality in the workman, and his apparent hopeless enslavement to his profit-grinding master, stimulated the hopes of civilization; probably more hymns have been sung in praise of division of labour, more sermons preached about it, than have done homage to the precept, "do unto others as ye would they should do unto you."

To drop all irony, surely this was one of those stages of civilization at which one might well say that, if it was to stop there, it was a pity that it had ever got so far. I have had to study books and methods of work of the eighteenth century a good deal, French chiefly; and I must say that the impression made on me by that study is that the eighteenth-century artisan must have been a terrible product of civilization, and quite in a condition to give rise to *hopes*—of the torch, the pike, and the guillotine.

However, civilization was not going to stop there; having turned the man into a machine, the next stage for commerce to aim at was to contrive machines which would widely dispense with human labour; nor was this aim altogether disappointed.

Now, at first sight it would seem that having got the workman into such a plight as he was, as the slave of division of labour, this new invention of machines which should free him from a part of his labour at least, could be nothing to him but an unmixed blessing. Doubtless it will prove to have been so in the end, when certain institutions have been swept away which most people now look on as eternal; but a longish time has passed during which the workman's hopes of civilization have been disappointed, for those who invented the machines, or rather who profited by their invention, did not aim at the saving of labour in the sense of reducing the labour which each man had to do, but, first taking it for granted that every workman would have to work as long as he could stand up to it, aimed, under those conditions of labour, at producing the utmost possible amount of goods which they could sell at a profit.

Need I dwell on the fact that, under these circumstances, the invention of the machines has benefited the workman but little even to this day?

Nay, at first they made his position worse than it had been: for, being thrust on the world very suddenly, they distinctly brought about an industrial revolution, changing everything suddenly and completely; industrial productiveness was increased prodigiously, but so far from the workers reaping the benefit of this, they were thrown out of work in enormous numbers, while those who were still employed were reduced from the position of skilled artisans to that of unskilled labourers: the aims of their masters being, as I said, to make a profit, they did not trouble themselves about this as a class, but took it for granted that it was something that couldn't be helped and didn't hurt *them:* nor did they think of offering to the workers that compensation for harassed interests which they have since made a point of claiming so loudly for themselves.

This was the state of things which followed on the conclusion of European peace, and even that peace itself rather made matters worse than better, by the sudden cessation of all war industries, and the throwing on to the market many thousands of soldiers and sailors: in short, at no period of English history was the condition of the workers worse than in the early years of the nineteenth century.

There seem during this period to have been two currents of hope that had reference to the working classes: the first affected the masters, the second the men.

In England, and, in what I am saying of this period, I am chiefly thinking of England, the hopes of the richer classes ran high; and no wonder; for England had by this time become the mistress of the markets of the world, and also, as the people of that period were never weary of boasting, the workshop of the world: the increase in the riches of the country was enormous, even at the early period I am thinking of now—prior to '48, I mean— though it increased much more speedily in times that we have all seen: but part of the jubilant hopes of this newly rich man concerned his servants, the instruments of his fortune: it was hoped that the population in general would grow wiser, better educated, thriftier, more in- dustrious, more comfortable; for which hope there was surely some foundation, since man's mastery over the forces of Nature was growing yearly towards completion; but you see these benevolent gentlemen supposed that these hopes would be realized perhaps by some unexplained magic as aforesaid, or perhaps by the working classes, *at their own expense,* by the exercise of virtues supposed to be specially suited to their condition, and called, by their masters, "thrift" and "industry." For this latter supposition there was no foundation: indeed, the poor wretches who were thrown out of work by the triumphant march of commerce had perforce worn thrift threadbare, and could hardly better their exploits in *that* direction; while as to those who worked in the factories, or who formed the fringe of labour elsewhere, industry was no new gospel to them, since they already worked as long as they could work without dying at the loom, the spindle, or the stithy. They for their part had their hopes, vague enough as to their ultimate aim, but expressed in the passing day by a very obvious tendency to revolt: this tendency took various forms, which I cannot dwell on here, but settled down at last into Chartism: about which I must speak a few words. But first I must mention, I can scarce do more, the honoured name of Robert Owen, as representative of the nobler hopes of his day, just as More was of his, and the lifter of the torch of Socialism amidst the dark days of the confusion consequent on the reckless greed of the early period of the great factory industries.

That the conditions under which man lived could affect his life and his deeds infinitely, that not selfish greed and ceaseless contention, but brotherhood and co-operation were the bases of true society, was the gospel which he preached and also practised with a single-heartedness, devotion, and fervour of hope which have never been surpassed: he was the embodied hope of the days when the advance of knowledge and the sufferings of the people thrust revolutionary hope upon those thinkers who were not in some form or other in the pay of the sordid masters of society.

As to the Chartist agitation, there is this to be said of it, that it was thoroughly a working-class movement, and it was caused by the simplest and most powerful of all causes—

hunger. It is noteworthy that it was strongest, especially in its earlier days, in the Northern and Midland manufacturing districts—that is, in the places which felt the distress caused by the industrial revolution most sorely and directly: it sprang up with particular vigour in the years immediately following the great Reform Bill; and it has been remarked that disappointment of the hopes which that measure had cherished had something to do with its bitterness. As it went on, obvious causes for failure were developed in it, self-seeking leadership; futile discussion of the means of making the change, before organization of the party was perfected; blind fear of ultimate consequences on the part of some, blind disregard to immediate consequences on the part of others; these were the surface reasons for its failure: but it would have triumphed over all these and accomplished revolution in England, if it had not been for causes deeper and more vital than these. Chartism differed from mere Radicalism in being a class movement; but its aim was after all political rather than social. The Socialism of Robert Owen fell short of its object because it did not understand that, as long as there is a privileged class in possession of the executive power, they will take good care that their economical position, which enables them to live on the unpaid labour of the people, is not tampered with: the hopes of the Chartists were disappointed because they did not understand that true political freedom is impossible to people who are economically enslaved: there is no first and second in these matters, the two must go hand in hand together: we cannot live as we will, and as we should, as long as we allow people to *govern* us whose interest it is that we should live as *they* will, and by no means as we should; neither is it any use claiming the right to manage our own business unless we are prepared to have some business of our own: these two aims united mean the furthering of the class struggle till all classes are abolished—the divorce of one from the other is fatal to any hope of social advancement.

Chartism therefore, though a genuine popular movement,

was incomplete in its aims and knowledge; the time was not yet come and it could not triumph openly; but it would be a mistake to say that it failed utterly: at least it kept alive the holy flame of discontent; it made it possible for us to attain to the political goal of democracy, and thereby to advance the cause of the people by the gain of a stage from whence could be seen the fresh gain to be aimed at.

I have said that the time for revolution had not then come: the great wave of commercial success went on swelling, and though the capitalists would if they had dared have engrossed the whole of the advantages thereby gained at the expense of their wage slaves, the Chartist revolt warned them that it was not safe to attempt it. They were *forced* to try to allay discontent by palliative measures. They had to allow Factory Acts to be passed regulating the hours and conditions of labour of women and children, and consequently of men also in some of the more important and consolidated industries; they were *forced* to repeal the ferocious laws against combination among the workmen; so that the Trades Unions won for themselves a legal position and became a power in the labour question, and were able by means of strikes and threats of strikes to regulate the wages granted to the workers, and to raise the standard of livelihood for a certain part of the skilled workmen and the labourers associated with them; though the main part of the unskilled, including the agricultural workmen, were no better off than before.

Thus was damped down the flame of a discontent vague in its aims, and passionately crying out for what, if granted, it could not have used: twenty years ago any one hinting at the possibility of serious class discontent in this country would have been looked upon as a madman; in fact, the well-to-do and cultivated were quite unconscious (as many still are) that there was any class distinction in this country other than what was made by the rags and cast clothes of feudalism, which in a perfunctory manner they still attacked.

There was no sign of revolutionary feeling in England

twenty years ago: the middle class were so rich that they had no need to hope for anything—but a heaven which they did not believe in: the well-to-do working men did not hope, since they were not pinched and had no means of learning their degraded position: and lastly, the drudges of the proletariat had such hope as charity, the hospital, the workhouse, and kind death at last could offer them.

In this stock-jobbers' heaven let us leave our dear countrymen for a little, while I say a few words about the affairs of the people on the continent of Europe. Things were not quite so smooth for the fleecer there: Socialist thinkers and writers had arisen about the same time as Robert Owen; St. Simon, Proudhon, Fourier and his followers kept up the traditions of hope in the midst of a *bourgeois* world. Amongst these Fourier is the one that calls for most attention: since his doctrine of the necessity and possibility of making labour attractive is one which Socialism can by no means do without. France also kept up the revolutionary and insurrectionary tradition, the result of something like hope still fermenting amongst the proletariat: she fell at last into the clutches of a second Cæsarism developed by the basest set of sharpers, swindlers, and harlots that ever insulted a country, and of whom our own happy *bourgeois* at home made heroes and heroines; the hideous open corruption of Parisian society, to which, I repeat, our respectable classes accorded heartfelt sympathy, was finally swept away by the horrors of a race war: the defeats and disgraces of this war developed, on the one hand, an increase in the wooden implacability and baseness of the French *bourgeois,* but on the other made way for revolutionary hope to spring again, from which resulted the attempt to establish society on the basis of the freedom of labour, which we call the Commune of Paris 1871. Whatever mistakes or imprudences were made in this attempt, and all wars blossom thick with such mistakes, I will leave the reactionary enemies of the people's cause to put forward: the immediate and obvious result was the slaughter of thousands of brave and honest revolutionists at the hands of the respectable classes, the loss in fact of an army for the popular cause. But we may be sure that the results of the Commune will not stop there: to all Socialists that heroic attempt will give hope and ardour in the cause as long as it is to be won; we feel as though the Paris work-man had striven to being the day-dawn for us, and had lifted us the sun's rim over the horizon, never to set in utter darkness again: of such attempts one must say, that though those who perished in them might have been put in a better place in the battle, yet after all brave men never die for nothing, when they die for principle.

Let us shift from France to Germany before we get back to England again, and conclude with a few words about our hopes at the present day. To Germany we owe the school of economists, at whose head stands the name of Karl Marx, who have made modern Socialism what it is: the earlier Socialist writers and preachers based their hopes on man being taught to see the desirableness of cooperation taking the place of competition, and adopting the change voluntarily and consciously, and they trusted to schemes more or less artificial being tried and accepted, although such schemes were necessarily constructed out of the mate-rials which capitalistic society offered: but the new school, starting with an historical view of what had been, and seeing that a law of evolution swayed all events in it, was able to point out to us that the evolution was still going on, and that, whether Socialism be desirable or not, it is at least inevitable. Here then was at last a hope of a different kind to any that had gone before it; and the German and Austrian workmen were not slow to learn the lesson found-ed on this theory; from being one of the most backward countries in Europe in the movement, before Lassalle start-ed his German workman's party in 1863, Germany soon became the leader in it: Bismarck's repressive law has only acted on opinion there, as the roller does to the growing grass—made it firmer and stronger; and whatever vicissi-tudes may be the fate of the party as a party, there can be no doubt that Socialistic opinion is firmly established there, and that when the time is ripe for it that opinion will express itself in action.

Now, in all I have been saying, I have been wanting you to trace the fact that, ever since the establishment of commercialism on the ruins of feudality, there has been growing a steady feeling on the part of the workers that they are a class dealt with as a class, and in like manner to deal with others; and that as this class feeling has grown, so also has grown with it a consciousness of the antagonism between their class and the class which employs it, as the phrase goes; that is to say, which lives by means of its labour.

Now it is just this growing consciousness of the fact that as long as there exists in society a propertied class living on the labour of a propertyless one, there *must* be a struggle always going on between those two classes—it is just the dawning knowledge of this fact which should show us what civilization can hope for—namely, transformation into true society, in which there will no longer be classes with their necessary struggle for existence and superiority: for the antagonism of classes which began in all simplicity between the master and the chattel slave of ancient society, and was continued between the feudal lord and the serf of mediæval society, has gradually become the contention between the capitalist developed from the workmen of the last-named period, and the wage-earner; in the former struggle the rise of the artisan and villenage tenant created a new class, the middle class, while the place of the old serf was filled by the propertyless labourer, with whom the middle class, which has absorbed the aristocracy, is now face to face: the struggle between the classes therefore is once again a simple one, as in the days of the classical peoples; but since there is no longer any strong race left out of civilization, as in the time of the disruption of Rome, the whole struggle in all its simplicity between those who have and those who lack is *within* civilization.

Moreover, the capitalist or modern slave-owner has been forced by his very success, as we have seen, to organize his slaves, the wage-earners, into a co-operation for production so well arranged that it requires little but his own elimination to make it a foundation for communal life: in the teeth also of the experience of past ages, he has been compelled to allow a modicum of education to the propertyless, and has not even been able to deprive them wholly of political rights; his own advance in wealth and power has bred for him the very enemy who is doomed to make an end of him.

But will there be any new class to take the place of the present proletariat when that has triumphed, as it must do, over the present privileged class? We cannot foresee the future, but we may fairly hope not: at least we cannot see any signs of such a new class forming. It is impossible to see how destruction of privilege can stop short of absolute equality of condition; pure Communism is the logical deduction from the imperfect form of the new society, which is generally differentiated from it as Socialism.

Meantime, it is this simplicity and directness of the growing contest which above all things presents itself as a terror to the conservative instinct of the present day. Many among the middle class who are sincerely grieved and shocked at the condition of the proletariat which civilization has created, and even alarmed by the frightful inequalities which it fosters, do nevertheless shudder back from the idea of the class struggle, and strive to shut their eyes to the fact that it is going on. They try to think that peace is not only possible, but natural, between the two classes, the very essence of whose existence is that each can only thrive by what it manages to force the other to yield to it. They propose to themselves the impossible problem of raising the inferior or exploited classes into a position in which they will cease to struggle against the superior classes, while the latter will not cease to exploit them. This absurd position drives them into the concoction of schemes for bettering the condition of the working classes at their own expense, some of them futile, some merely fantastic; or they may be divided again into those which point out the advantages and pleasures of involuntary asceticism, and reactionary plans for importing the conditions of the production and life of the Middle Ages (wholly misunderstood by them, by the way) into the present system of the capitalist farmer, the great industries, and the universal world-market. Some see a solution of the social problem in sham co-operation, which is merely an improved form of joint-stockery: others preach thrift to (precarious) incomes of eighteen shillings a week, and industry to men killing themselves by inches in working overtime, or to men whom the labour-market has rejected as not wanted: others beg the proletarians not to breed so fast; an injunction the compliance with which might be at first of advantage to the proletarians themselves in their present condition, but would certainly undo the capitalists, if it were carried to any lengths, and would lead through ruin and misery to the violent outbreak of the very revolution which these timid people are so anxious to forego.

Then there are others who, looking back on the past, and perceiving that the workmen of the Middle Ages lived in more comfort and self-respect than ours do, even though they were subjected to the class rule of men who were looked on as another order of beings than they, think that if those conditions of life could be reproduced under our better political conditions the question would be solved for a time at least. Their schemes may be summed up in attempts, more or less preposterously futile, to graft a class of independent peasants on our system of wages and capital. They do not understand that this system of independent workmen, producing almost entirely for the consumption of themselves and their neighbours, and exploited by the upper classes by obvious taxes on their labour, which was not otherwise organized or interfered with by the exploiters, was what in past times took the place of our system, in which the workers sell their labour in the competitive market to masters who have in their hands the whole organization of the markets, and that these two systems are mutually destructive.

Others again believe in the possibility of starting from

our present workhouse system, for the raising of the lowest part of the working population into a better condition, but do not trouble themselves as to the position of the workers who are fairly above the condition of pauperism, or consider what part they will play in the contest for a better livelihood. And, lastly, quite a large number of well-intentioned persons belonging to the richer classes believe, that in a society that compels competition for livelihood, and holds out to the workers as a stimulus to exertion the hope of their rising into a monopolist class of nonproducers, it is yet possible to "moralize" capital (to use a slang phrase of the Positivists): that is to say, that a sentiment imported from a religion which looks upon another world as the true sphere of action for mankind, will override the necessities of our daily life in this world. This curious hope is founded on the feeling that a sentiment antagonistic to the full development of commercialism exists and is gaining ground, and that this sentiment is an independent growth of the ethics of the present epoch. As a matter of fact, admitting its existence, as I think we must do, it is the birth of the sense of insecurity which is the shadow cast before by the approaching dissolution of modern society founded on wage-slavery.

The greater part of these schemes aim, though seldom with the consciousness of their promoters, at the creation of a new middle class out of the wage-earning class, and at their expense, just as the present middle class was developed out of the serf-population of the early Middle Ages. It may be possible that such a *further* development of the middle class lies before us, but it will not be brought about by any such artificial means as the above mentioned schemes. If it comes at all, it must be produced by events, which at present we cannot foresee, acting on our commercial system, and revivifying for a little time, maybe, that Capitalist Society which now seems sickening towards its end.

For what is visible before us in these days is the competitive commercial system killing itself by its own force:

profits lessening, business growing bigger and bigger, the small employer of labour thrust out of his function, and the aggregation of capital increasing the numbers of the lower middle class from above rather than from below, by driving the smaller manufacturer into the position of a mere servant to the bigger. The productivity of labour also increasing out of all proportion to the capacity of the capitalists to manage the market or deal with the labour supply: lack of employment therefore becoming chronic, and discontent therewithal.

All this on the one hand. On the other, the workman claiming everywhere political equality, which cannot long be denied; and education spreading, so that what between the improvement in the education of the working class and the continued amazing fatuity of that of the upper classes, there is a distinct tendency to equalization here; and, as I have hinted above, all history shows us what a danger to society may be a class at once educated and socially degraded: though, indeed, no history has yet shown us—what is swiftly advancing upon us—a class which, though it shall have attained knowledge, shall lack utterly the refinement and self-respect which come from the union of knowledge with leisure and ease of life. The growth of such a class may well make the "cultured" poeple of to-day tremple.

Whatever, therefore, of unforeseen and unconceived-of may lie in the womb of the future, there is nothing visible before us but a decaying system, with no outlook but ever-increasing entanglement and blindness, and a new system, Socialism, the hope of which is ever growing clearer in men's minds—a system which not only sees how labour can be freed from its present fetters, and organized unwastefully, so as to produce the greatest possible amount of wealth for the community and for every member of it, but which bears with it its own ethics and religion and æsthetics: that is the hope and promise of a new and higher life in all ways. So that even if those unforeseen economical events above spoken of were to happen, and put off for a while the end of our Capitalist system, the latter would drag itself along as an anomaly cursed by all, a mere clog on the aspirations of humanity.

It is not likely that it will come to that: in all probability the logical outcome of the latter days of Capitalism will go step by step with its actual history: while all men, even its declared enemies, will be working to bring Socialism about, the aims of those who have learned to believe in the certainty and beneficence of its advent will become clearer, their methods for realizing it clearer also, and at last ready to hand. Then will come that open acknowledgment for the necessity of the change (an acknowledgment coming from the intelligence of civilization) which is commonly called Revolution. It is no use prophesying as to the events which will accompany that revolution, but to a reasonable man it seems unlikely to the last degree, or we will say impossible, that a moral sentiment will induce the proprietary classes—those who live by *owning* the means of production which the unprivileged classes must needs *use*—to yield up this privilege uncompelled; all one can hope is that they will see the implicit threat of compulsion in the events of the day, and so yield with a good grace to the terrible necessity of forming part of a world in which all, including themselves, will work honestly and live easily.

TWO LETTERS
TO JANE ALICE MORRIS

[From *The Letters of William Morris*, edited by Philip Henderson, 269-73.

Jane was Morris' elder daughter, and, though suffering from poor health, was perhaps more fully in sympathy with his ideas than any other member of the family. These letters, giving a vivid picture of his day-to-day work in the movement, help to explain why he was both respected and loved.]

Hammersmith
14 April [1887]

I came back later from Scotland and the north than I had intended; otherwise you would have heard from me before; I found your letter for me on Tuesday evening last, which was a great pleasure to me dear.

Well as to the adventures of a respectable Socialist preacher, they are not very exciting (which is a good job) but they are perhaps of some interest.

I got to Glasgow on Sunday morning April 3 and was very glad of my wash and breakfast. I had to sleep at the Hotel that night Comrade Muirhead not being ready to give me guesting. Well I began operations by helping the ordinary open-air meeting in Jail Square (ominous name) which is just in front of a doleful openish garden called the Green: a meeting much like ours in London a good one of its kind: then we had a meeting of the Branch at their rooms and found them in a solid satisfactory condition: I rather blushed by the way to see my name in such large letters on the walls, as their posters were enormous, the League badge enlarged at the top of them: then in the evening came the lecture: my M.P.[1] really turning up as

1 He was R. B. Cunninghame Graham (1852–1936), author, traveller, Socialist, M. P. North Lanarkshire, 1886–92.

chairman, which in Scotland requires some courage: the meeting was very good upwards of a thousand people though they had to pay. The lecture was new, I was in good condition and the audience was very hearty and took up the points well, and we carried the Socialist resolution easily. Next day to Dundee under the wing of a parson turned out of the church for not believing in damnation, and who has set up for himself. A good audience as to numbers—but more or less the parson's congregation: also I was only part of the entertainment; music (which if it had been good I should not have objected to) being part of it also: however I was on my metal & got a good deal into my 40 minutes speech. So across the water of Tay to parson's house: an architect went with us who much belied his name of "Stark" but I forgive [him] for the admiration he expressed of Brampton church, which he had stumbled across. I forgot to say that young Steggall made a speech, & not a bad one. Next morning it snowed heavily for 3 hours, but I was not snowed up as I expected to be: the place on the water side looking on Dundee and its "Law" or hill was very beautiful. So to Edinburgh with a nice innocent comrade of that branch "Gilray" who dropped in upon me the day before: You know one has about 20 minutes sea from Fife across the firth to Granton, whence of old time I set sail for Iceland. I stayed with Glasse at Edinburgh and had a meeting in the evening (Tuesday 5th) not very well attended, but interesting because it seems the audience was a new one, and a good [deal] hostile so that Glasse was afraid of putting our resolution, which however we carried after a rather stormy debate, owing to the stupidity of a cut and dried opponent one Job Bone, who always opposes everything and is known in Edinburgh as the "Bone of Contention". Well next day I went to Glasgow again; only I stopped at Linlithgow on the way, where there is the 15th century palace, a ruin, but nearly complete on the border of a little lake, and a fine church the nave quite untouched, the choir made very ugly by the presbyterian fittings, and stupid by a feeble attempt at restoration. Then in the evening was a party of the Branch rather slow; our Scotch friends not being very good at that sort of thing they are so shy. The next day (Thursday) I went to Hamilton the heart of the coalmining district; the poor miners have just gone in again there, and are very depressed and wretched and our meeting was but a small one (it would have been better in the open air) but whatever was there was heartily on our side: except a drunken man in the gallery who persisted in taking me for Mr Mason his M.P. and quarrelling with me on some political subject to which I had never alluded. On the Friday I went to Paisley where we had a fairish meeting in a big hall: the audience attentive rather than enthusiastic; however we took 6 or 7 names for a new branch: the provost (mayor in England) took the chair for me: a little old body who had been an advanced man some 50 years ago in the old Chartist times when Paisley was (as it is now) a very radical town. A doleful place to look at, but with the nave of the old abbey church yet left, a fine 13th century building, which must have been very fine indeed when its long aisleless choir was still standing, of which but a few walls are left. This was to have finished my work; but on the Wednesday I had heard from the London comrades begging me to go to Mahon's help at Newcastle, as he has been carrying on a very successful campaign amongst the miners thereabout and was to have a big meeting on Easter Monday: so I yea said that and stayed on the Saturday and Sunday at Glasgow; on Saturday we went to Coatbridge and held an open air meeting there; 'tis an iron working place where at night the flaring furnaces put out the moon and stars: the men are seldom out of work there; but work 7 days a week in this Devil's Den: Sunday *working* not seeming to hurt the Scotch conscience though Sunday playing does. There we were in rivalry with the Salvation Army and a cheap-jack, but had a good meeting only disturbed by a drunken Irish man, who insisted with many oaths on our telling him the difference between a Home-Ruler and a non-Home-Ruler, and swore by Christ that *he* would teach us Socialism *he* would: but the crowd soon put him down. All this we did by star and furnace light, which was strange and even dreadful.

Sunday afternoon I said goodbye to Glasgow to a large audience on the Green who were very sympathetic; but sadly poor & pinched they look as they well may. I went off to Newcastle in the evening & found Mahon and Donald there at 11 p.m.: also stumbled on Hyndman as the two bodies are working together there. But my paper is nearly done, & it is nearly post time: so I will write again presently & tell you my Northumberland adventures & send this off together with the Newcastle paper which will tell you some of them.

Hammersmith
23 April [1887]

Here is another scrawl for you; and first to begin where I left off. I got to Newcastle on Easter Sunday evening about 11 and found Mahon and Donald there: also I presently met Hyndman, who I suspect was not overpleased to see me, as the S.D.F. have been playing a rather mean game there; however I was taken to a temperance hotel for my lodging, not I suppose because I was thought likely to get drunk, but because such places are quieter & cleaner than the third-rate other hotels. Early the next morning we started off for the collieries, and alighted from the train in a wretched-looking country enough; not smoky, for alack the collieries are not working, but so waste and desolate looking like—well a "back yard" on a large scale. The roads of course were black and presently we had to strike off onto a railway which was also a footpath and went through one of the collieries; this brought us out presently into the "village" where the pitmen lived called Seghill where Mahon had a great following, and then we went into one of our friend's houses. The family were all in, a man, his wife & daughter: they were very nice people, the man intelligent & pleasant, talking with that queer Northumbrian smack that makes the talk sound

like that of foreigners; poor man, he had lost one eye in
an accident & damaged the other; the house was as clean
and neat as a country cottage, and indeed they all seemed
like that; most of them as we passed their open doors
showed a swell but ugly bedstead in the place of honour:
Well Donald & I sat and talked there while Mahon went
to make arrangements for these people to march to the
field where the meeting was to be: and after about an hour
we went to the railway station & Mahon & I set off for
Blithe where we were to pick up another detachment:
when we all got to the station there we found quite a
crowd waiting for us who followed us to the market-place,
& as Mahon again had some arrangements to make they
brought a trolly to the place & I got up and amused them
by a speech of some half hour or more: then we set off,
rather a draggle-tailed lot because we couldn't afford a
paid band, and so hadn't got one there, and not more than
half the men in the market-place followed us, and we
straggled a good deal.

Blithe is a sea-port, and as we came in I could see the
masts of ships there: and as we plodded on through the
dreary (O so dreary) villages, & that terrible waste of end-
less back-yard, we could see on our left hand a strip of
the bright blue sea, for it was a beautiful sunny day. At
last at one village we saw a crowd drawn up and a band
& a "banner," and then we fell into some sort of order
and rolled up rapidly, so we went on till we mounted the
crest of a low hill after a 6 mile march and had some 2000
at our heels by then. We came on to the meeting field
where the two other detachments had already come, and
besides groups of men and women were streaming up the
field from all about: the crowd was thick about the
waggon we were to speak from, & a most orderly & good-
tempered crowd at that: but when we were all in and they
saw the reporters there also, they sang out "put those chaps
(the reporters) out unless they promise to put all down!"
There were many women there, some of them very much
excited: one (elderly) when any obnoxious person was

named never failed to chorus it with "put him out!": all near the waggon the men all sat down on the ground to give the others a chance to hear: We had to stand on a rather perilous plank above the rail of the waggon, & I was for simply coming to the front without mounting on the plank but some of them sung out from the side, "If yon man does na stand on the top we canna hear him!" So up I had to climb: however some one turned a poled notice board up for me and I leaned on that and so was pretty comfortable. It was very inspiriting to speak to such a big crowd of eager & serious persons, and I did pretty well and didn't stumble at all.

Well that meeting over we three had to rush for the train to Newcastle, as we were to speak at another place in the evening: we just caught the train, and got into Newcastle about 6 p.m. properly hungry, I for one; and so off we went to the big station & into the refreshment room, where as we were stowing the victuals into us who should come up but Joseph Cowen very friendly & nice, I must say, and we had a talk, all we could in twenty minutes space. Then off we went to Ryton Willows, which is even now a pretty place on the side of the Tyne; it is a recreation ground and being Easter Monday there were lots of folk there with swings and cricket and dancing & the like: I thought it a queer place for a serious Socialist meeting, but we had a crowd about us in no time and I spoke, rather too long I fancy, till the stars came out and it grew dusk and the people stood and listened still, & when we were done they gave three cheers for the Socialists, & all was mighty friendly & pleasant: & so back we went to supper and bed, of which I for one was glad enough. However I felt very well & brisk next morning, and so got up to town in time to get to our Council meeting, and arrange for a meeting in Hyde Park which is to come off to-morrow to sympathize with the miners. So much for my adventures, my dear, which are not very adventurous, but I know that you like to hear what I am about.

THE SOCIETY OF THE FUTURE

[A lecture delivered to the Hammersmith Branch of the Socialist League on November 13th, 1887—the evening of Bloody Sunday. May Morris, II, 453-68.

It is worth remembering that the events of this day, described in the next item, played an important part in shaping Morris' ideas of how revolution might begin in England, as described in Chapter XVII of *News from Nowhere*.]

IN making our claims for the changes in Society which we believe would set labour free and thus bring about a new Society, we Socialists are satisfied with demanding what we think necessary for that Society to form itself, which we are sure it is getting ready to do; this we think better than putting forward elaborate utopian schemes for the future. We assert that monopoly must come to an end, and that those who can use the means of the production of wealth should have all opportunity of doing so, without being forced to surrender a great part of the wealth which they have created to an irresponsible owner of the necessaries to production; and we have faith in the regenerative qualities of this elementary piece of honesty, and believe that the world thus set free will enter on a new cycle of progress. We are prepared to face whatever drawbacks may accompany this new devolopment with equanimity, being convinced that it will at any rate be a great gain to have got rid of a system which has at last become nearly all drawbacks. The extinction of the disabilities of an effete system of production will not, we are convinced, destroy the gains which the world has already won, but will, on the contrary, make those gains available to the whole population instead of confining their enjoyment to a few. In short, considering the present condition of the world, we have come to the conclusion that the function of the reformers now alive is not so much prophecy as action. It is our business to use the means ready to our hands to remedy the immediate evils which oppress us; to the coming generations we must leave the task of safeguarding and of using the freedom which our efforts shall have won them.

Nevertheless, we do partly know the direction which the development of the world will take in the immediate future; the evolution of past history teaches us that. We know that the world cannot go back on its footsteps, and that men will develop swiftly both bodily and mentally in the new Society; we know that men in general will feel the obligations of Society much more than the latter generations have done, that the necessity for co-operation in production and life in general will be more consciously felt than it has been; that the comparative ease of life which the freeing of labour will bring about will give all men more leisure and time for thought; that crime will be rarer because there will not be the same temptation to it; that increased ease of life and education combined will tend to free us from disease of body and mind. In short, that the world cannot take a step forward in justice, honesty and kindliness, without a corresponding gain in all the material conditions of life.

And besides what we know, a knowledge without which we should not take the trouble to agitate for a change in the basis of Society, we cannot help guessing at a great deal which we cannot know; and again, this guessing, these hopes, or if you will, these dreams for the future, make many a man a Socialist whom sober reason deduced from science and political economy and the selection of the fittest would not move at all. They put a man in a fit frame of mind to study the reasons for his hope; give him courage to wade through studies, which, as the Arab king said of arithmetic, would otherwise be too dull for the mind of man to think of.

There are, in fact, two groups of mind with whom Social Revolutionists like other people have to deal, the analytical and the constructive. Belonging to the latter group myself, I am fully conscious of the dangers which we incur, and still more perhaps of the pleasures which we lose, and am, I hope, duly grateful to the more analytical minds for their setting of us straight when our yearning for action leads us astray, and I am also, I confess, somewhat envious of the beatitude of their dreamy contemplation of the perfection of some favourite theory; a happiness which we who use our eyes more than our reasoning powers for noting what is going on in the world, seldom or never enjoy.

However, as they would and do call our instinctive vision dreaming, and as they almost always, at least in their own estimation, have the better of us in argument when we meet in friendly battle, I must be careful what I say of them, and so will for the present at least only deal with the visionaries or *practical people*. And one thing I must confess from the beginning, which is that the visions of us visionary or practical people differ largely from each other, and that we are not much interested in each other's visions; whereas the theories of the analysts differ little from each other, and they are hugely interested in each others' theories—in the way that a butcher is interested in an ox—to wit, for cutting up.

So I will not attempt to compare my visions with those of other Socialists, but will simply talk to you of some of my own, and let you make the comparison yourselves, those of you who are visionaries, or let you unassisted by me criticize them, those of you who are analytically given. In short, I am going to give you a chapter of confessions. I want to tell you what it is I desire of the Society of the Future, just as if I were going to be reborn into it; I daresay that you will find some of my visions strange enough.

One reason which will make some of you think them strange is a sad and shameful one. I have always belonged to the well-to-do classes, and was born into luxury, so that necessarily I ask much more of the future than many of you do; and the first of all my visions, and that which colours all my others, is of a day when that misunderstanding will no longer be possible; when the words poor and rich, though they will still be found in our dictionaries, will have lost their old meaning; which will have to be explained with care by great men of the analytical kind, spending much time and many words over the job, and not succeeding in the end in making people do more than pretend to understand them.

Well now, to begin with, I am bound to suppose that the realization of Socialism will tend to make men happy. What is it then makes people happy? Free and full life and the consciousness of life. Or, if you will, the pleasurable exercise of our energies, and the enjoyment of the rest which that exercise or expenditure of energy makes necessary to us. I think that is happiness for all, and covers all difference of capacity and temperament from the most energetic to the laziest.

Now, whatever interferes with that freedom and fulness of life, under whatever specious guise it may come, is an evil; is something to be got rid of as speedily as possible. It ought not to be endured by reasonable men, who naturally wish to be happy.

Here you see is an admission on my part which I suspect indicates the unscientific mind. It proposes the exercise of free will on the part of men, which the latest scientists deny the possibility of, I believe; but don't be afraid, I am not going into argument on the matter of free will and predestination; I am only going to assert that if individual men are the creatures of their surrounding conditions, as indeed I think they are, it must be the business of man as a social animal, or of Society, if you will, to make the surroundings which make the individual man what he is. Man must and does create the conditions under which he lives; let him be conscious of that, and create them wisely.

Has he done so hitherto? He has tried to do so, I think,

but with only moderate success, at any rate at times. However, the results of that moderate success he is proud of, and he calls it *civilization*. Now, there has been amongst people of different minds abundant discussion as to whether civilization is a good thing or an evil. Our friend Bax in his very able article on the subject, did, I think, really put the matter on its true footing when he pointed out that as a step to something better, civilization was a good, but as an achievement it was an evil. In that sense I declare myself an enemy of civilization; nay, since this is to be a chapter of confessions, I must tell you that my *special* leading motive as a Socialist is hatred of civilization; my ideal of the new Society would not be satisfied unless that Society destroyed civilization.

For if happiness be the pleasurable exercise of our energies and the enjoyment of necessary rest, it seems to me that civilization, looked at from the static point of view, as Bax phrases it, tends to deny us both these good things, and thereby tends to reduce man to a machine without a will; to deprive him gradually of all the functions of an animal and the pleasure of fulfilling them, except the most elementary ones. The scientific ideal of the future of man would appear to be an intellectual paunch, nourished by circumstances over which he has no control, and without the faculty of communicating the results of his intelligence to his brother-paunches.

Therefore my ideal of the Society of the future is first of all the freedom and cultivation of the individual will, which civilization ignores, or even denies the existence of; the shaking of the slavish dependence, not on other men, but on artificial systems made to save men manly trouble and responsibility: and in order that this will may be vigorous in us, I demand a free and unfettered animal life for man first of all: I demand the utter extinction of all asceticism. If we feel the least degradation in being amorous, or merry, or hungry, or sleepy, we are so far bad animals, and therefore miserable men. And you know civilization *does* bid us to be ashamed of all these moods and deeds, and as far as she can, begs us to conceal them, and where possible to get other people to do them for us. In fact, it seems to me that civilization may almost be defined as a system arranged for ensuring the vicarious exercise of human energies for a minority of privileged persons.

Well, but this demand for the extinction of asceticism bears with it another demand: for the extinction of luxury. Does that seem a paradox to you? It ought not to do so. What brings about luxury but a sickly discontent with the simple joys of the lovely earth? What is it but a warping of the natural beauty of things into a perverse ugliness to satisfy the jaded appetite of a man who is ceasing to be a man—a man who will not work, and cannot rest? Shall I tell you what luxury has done for you in modern Europe? It has covered the merry green fields with the hovels of slaves, and blighted the flowers and trees with poisonous gases, and turned the rivers into sewers; till over many parts of Britain the common people have forgotten what a field or a flower is like, and their idea of beauty is a gas-poisoned gin-palace or a tawdry theatre. And civilization thinks that is all right, and it doesn't heed it; and the rich man practically thinks, 'Tis all right, the common people are used to it now, and so long as they can fill their bellies with the husks that the swine do eat, it is enough. And all for what? To have fine pictures painted, beautiful buildings built, good poems written? O no: those are the deeds of the ages before luxury, before civilization. Luxury rather builds clubs in Pall Mall, and upholsters them as though for delicate invalid ladies, for the behoof of big whiskered men, that they may lounge there amidst such preposterous effeminacy that the very plushed-breeched flunkies that wait upon the loungers are better men than they are. I needn't go further than that: a grand club is the very representative of luxury.

Well, you see I dwell upon that matter of luxury, which is really the sworn foe of pleasure, because I don't want workmen even temporarily to look upon a swell club as a desirable thing. I know how difficult it is for them to look from out of their poverty and squalor to a life of real and manly pleasure; but I ask them to think that the good life of the future will be as little like the life of the present rich as may be: that life of the rich is only the wrong side of their own misery; and surely since it is the cause of the misery, there can be nothing enviable or desirable in it. When our opponents say, as they sometimes do, How should we be able to procure the luxuries of life in a Socialist society? answer boldly, We could not do so, and we don't care, for we don't want them and won't have them; and indeed, I feel sure that we cannot if we are all free men together. Free men, I am sure, must lead simple lives and have simple pleasures: and if we shudder away from that necessity now, it is because we are not free men, and have in consequence wrapped up our lives in such a complexity of dependence that we have grown feeble and helpless. But again, what is simplicity? Do you think by chance that I mean a row of yellow-brick, blue-slated houses, or a phalangstère like an improved Peabody lodging-house; and the dinner-bell ringing one into a row of white basins of broth with a piece of bread cut nice and square by each, with boiler-made tea and ill boiled rice-pudding to follow? No; that's the philanthropist's ideal, not mine; and here I only note it to repudiate it, and to say, Vicarious life once more, and therefore no pleasure. No, I say; find out what you yourselves find pleasant, and do it. You won't be alone in your desires; you will get plenty to help you in carrying them out, and you will develop social life in developing your own special tendencies.

So, then, my ideal is first unconstrained life, and next simple and natural life. First you must be free; and next you must learn to take pleasure in all the details of life: which, indeed, will be necessary for you, because, since others will be free, you will have to do your own work. That is in direct opposition to civilization, which says, Avoid trouble, which you can only do by making other people live your life for you. I say, Socialists ought to say,

Take trouble, and turn your trouble into pleasure: that I shall always hold is the key to a happy life.

Now let us try to use that key to unlock a few of the closed doors of the future: and you must remember, of course, in speaking of the Society of the future, I am taking the indulgence of passing over the transitional period— whatever that may be—that will divide the present from the ideal; which, after all, we must all of us more or less form in our minds when we have once fixed our belief in the regeneration of the world. And first as to the form of the position of people in the new Society—their political position, so to say. Political society as we know it will have come to an end: the relations between man and man will no longer be that of status or of property. It will no longer be the hierarchical position, the office of the man, that will be considered, as in the Middle Ages, nor his property as now, but his person. Contract enforced by the State will have vanished into the same limbo as the holiness of the nobility of blood. So we shall at one stroke get rid of all that side of artificiality which bids us sacrifice each our own life to the supposed necessity of an institution which is to take care of the troubles of people which may never happen: every case of clashing rights and desires will be dealt with on its own merits—that is, really, and not legally. Private property of course will not exist as a right: there will be such an abundance of all ordinary necessaries that between private persons there will be no obvious and immediate exchange necessary; though no one will want to meddle with matters that have as it were grown to such and such an individual—which have become part of his habits, so to say.

Now, as to occupations, we shall clearly not be able to have the same division of labour in them as now: vicarious servanting, sewer-emptying, butchering, letter-carrying, boot-blacking, hair-dressing, and the rest of it, will have come to an end: we shall either make all these occupations agreeable to ourselves in some mood or to some minds, who will take to them voluntarily, or we shall have to let them lapse altogether. A great many fidgety occupations will come to an end: we shan't put a pattern on a cloth or a twiddle on a jug-handle to sell it, but to make it prettier and to amuse ourselves and others. Whatever rough or inferior wares we make, will be made rough and inferior to perform certain functions of use, and not to sell: as there will be no slaves, there will be no use for wares which none but slaves would need. Machinery will probably to a great extent have served its purpose in allowing the workers to shake off privilege, and will I believe be much curtailed. Possibly the few more important machines will be very much improved, and the host of unimportant ones fall into disuse, and as to many or most of them, people will be able to use them or not as they feel inclined—as, e.g., if we want to go a journey we shall not be compelled to go by railway as we are now, in the interests of property, but may indulge our personal inclinations and travel in a tilted waggon or on the hindquarters of a donkey.

Again, the aggregation of the population having served *its* purpose of giving people opportunities of inter-communication and of making the workers feel their solidarity, will also come to an end; and the huge manufacturing districts will be broken up, and nature heal the horrible scars that man's heedless greed and stupid terror have made: for it will no longer be a matter of dire necessity that cotton cloth should be made a fraction of a farthing cheaper this year than last. It will be in our own choice whether we will work an extra half-hour a-day more to obtain a clean home and green fields; nor will the starvation or misery of thousands follow some slight caprice in the market for wares not worth making at all. Of course (as I ought to have said before) there are many ornamental matters which will be made privately in people's leisure hours, as they could easily be: since it is not the making of a real work of art that takes so much ingenuity as the making of a machine for the making of a makeshift. And of course mere cheating and flunky centres like the horrible muck-heap in which we dwell

(London, to wit) could be got rid of easier still; and a few pleasant villages on the side of the Thames might mark the place of that preposterous piece of folly once called London.

Now let us use the key to unlock the door of the education of the future. Our present education is purely commercial and political: we are none of us educated to be men, but some to be property-owners, and others to be property-servers. Again I demand the due results of revolution on the basis of non-ascetic simplicity of life. I think here also we must get rid of the fatal division-of-labour system. All people should learn how to swim, and to ride, and to sail a boat on sea or river; such things are not arts, they are merely bodily exercises, and should become habitual in the race; and also one or two elementary arts of life, as carpentry or smithying; and most should know how to shoe a horse and shear a sheep and reap a field and plough it (we should soon drop machinery in agriculture I believe when we were free). Then again there are things like cooking and baking, sewing, and the like, which can be taught to every sensible person in a few hours, and which everybody ought to have at his fingers' ends. All these elementary arts would be once again habitual, as also I suppose would be the arts of reading and writing; as also I suspect would the art of thinking, at present not taught in any school or university that I know of.

Well, armed with these habits and arts, life would lie before the citizen for him to enjoy; for whatever line he might like to take up for the exercise of his energies, he would find the community ready to help him with teaching, opportunities, and material. Nor for my part would I prescribe for him what he should do, being persuaded that the habits which would have given him the capacities of a man would stimulate him to use them; and that the process of the enjoyment of his life would be carried out, not at the expense of his fellow-citizens, but for their benefit. At present, you know, the gains held out as a stimulus to exertion, to all those who are not stimulated by the whip of the threat of death by starvation, are narrow, and are mainly the hope that the successfully energetic man shall be placed in a position where he shall not have to exercise his energies: the boredom of satiety, in short, is the crown of valiant exertion in civilization. But in a social condition of things, the gains that would lie before the exercise of one's energies would be various and wide indeed; nor do I in the least in the world believe that the possibility of mere personal use would, or indeed could, limit people's endeavour after them; since men would at last have recognized that it was their business to live, and would at once come to the conclusion that life without endeavour is *dull*. Now what direction that endeavour would take, of course I cannot tell you; I can only say that it would be set free from the sordid necessity to work at what doesn't please us, which is the besetting curse of civilization. The suggestion of a hope I may, however, make, which is of course personal—which is that perhaps mankind will regain their eyesight, which they have at present lost to a great extent. I am not here alluding to what I believe is also a fact, that the number of people of imperfect mechanical sight is increasing, but to what I suppose is connected with that fact, namely, that people have largely ceased to take in mental impressions through the eyes; whereas in times past the eyes were the great feeders of the fancy and imagination. Of course people use their eyes to prevent them from tumbling down stairs or from putting their forks to their noses instead of to their mouths, but there as a rule is an end of the use they are to people. I am in the habit when I go to an exhibition or a picture gallery of noticing their behaviour there; and as a rule I note that they seem very much bored, and their eyes wander vacantly over the various objects exhibited to them, and odd to say, a strange or unusual thing never attracts them, no doubt because it appeals to their minds chiefly through their eyes; whereas if they came across something which a printed label informs them is something familiar, they become interested and nudge each other. If, e.g., ordinary people go to our National

Gallery, the thing which they want to see is the Blenheim Raphael, which, though well done, is a very dull picture, at least to anyone not an artist; and they do this because they have been told that the—h'm! the—the—well, the thief that owned it managed to squeeze an exorbitant sum of money out of the nation for it. While, when Holbein shows them the Danish princess of the sixteenth century yet living on the canvas, the demure half-smile not yet faded from her eyes; when Van Eyck opens a window for them into Bruges of the fourteenth century; when Botticelli shows them Heaven as it lived in the hearts of men before theology was dead, these things produce no impression on them, not so much even as to stimulate their curiosity and make them ask what 'tis all about; because these things were done to be looked at, and to make the eyes tell the mind tales of the past, the present, and the future.

Or again, in times past, when what is (I suppose as a joke) called the Educational Department at South Kensington was more or less mixed up with the Art Department, I have followed up a group through the wonders of the drift of the art of past days, and perceived that their eyes never steadied once on any of these things, but that they brightened up at once when they came across a glass case in which the constituent parts of an analyzed beef-steak were neatly arranged and labelled, and that their eyes devoured little pinches of nothing in particular, with a trusting faith in the analyst which I confess I could not share, as it seemed to me that it would require a quite superhuman honesty in him not to snatch up a few pinches of road-dust or ashes and make them do duty for the recondite substances which his toil had brought to light in that familiar object. In literature you will find the same thing going on, and that those authors who appeal to our eyes to take in mental impressions are relegated by our most "intellectual" critics to a second place at least: to pass by Homer and Beowulf and Chaucer, you will find the "truly intellectual" man elevating mere rhetorical word-spinners and hunters of introspection above such masters of life as Scott and

Dickens, who tell their tales to our senses and leave them alone to moralize the tale so told.

Now I have dwelt at some length on this matter of the eyesight, because to my mind it is the most obvious sign of the march of civilization towards the intellectual-paunch stage of existence which I have deprecated already; and also because I feel sure that no special claim need be made for the art and literature of the future: healthy bodily conditions, a sound and all round development of the senses, joined to the due social ethics which the destruction of all slavery will give us, will, I am convinced, as a matter of course give us the due art and literature, whatever that due may turn out to be. Only, if I may prophesy ever so little, I should say that both art and literature, and especially art, will appeal to the senses directly, just as the art of the past has done. You see you will no longer be able to have novels relating the troubles of a middle-class couple in their struggle towards social uselessness, because the material for such literary treasures will have passed away. On the other hand the genuine tales of history will still be with us, and will, one might well hope, then be told in a cheerfuller strain than is now possible. Nor for my part can I doubt that art will appeal to the senses of men now grown healthy; which means that architecture and the kindred arts will again flourish amongst us as in the days before civilization. Civilization renders these arts impossible, because its politics and ethics force us to live in a grimy disorderly uncomfortable world, a world that offends the senses at every turn: that necessity reacts on the senses again, and forces us unconsciously to blunt their keenness. A man who otices the external forms of things much nowadays must suffer in South Lancashire or London, must live in a state of perpetual combat and anger; and he really must try to blunt his sensibility, or he will go mad, or kill some obnoxious person and be hanged for it; and this of course means that people will gradually get to be born without this inconvenient sensibility. On the other hand, let this irrational compulsion be removed from us, and the senses will grow again to their due and normal fulness and demand expression of the pleasure which their exercise gives us, which in short means art and literature at once sensuous and human.

Well, now I will try to draw these discursive remarks to a head, and will give you a more concise and complete idea of the society into which I would like to be reborn.

It is a society which does not know the meaning of the words rich and poor, or the rights of property, or law or legality, or nationality: a society which has no consciousness of being governed; in which equality of condition is a matter of course, and in which no man is rewarded for having served the community by having the power given him to injure it.

It is a society conscious of a wish to keep life simple, to forgo some of the power over nature won by past ages in order to be more human and less mechanical, and willing to sacrifice something to this end. It would be divided into small communities varying much within the limits allowed by due social ethics, but without rivalry between each other, looking with abhorrence at the idea of a holy race.

Being determined to be free, and therefore contented with a life not only simpler but even rougher than the life of slave-owners, division of labour would be habitually limited: men (and women too, of course) would do their work and take their pleasure in their own persons, and not vicariously: the social bond would be habitually and instinctively felt, so that there would be no need to be always asserting it by set forms: the family of blood-relationship would melt into that of the community and of humanity. The pleasures of such a society would be founded on the free exercise of the senses and passions of a healthy human animal, so far as this did not injure the other individuals of the community and so offend against social unity: no one would be ashamed of humanity or ask for anything better than its due development.

But from this healthy freedom would spring up the pleasures of intellectual development, which the men of civilisation so foolishly try to separate from sensuous life, and to glorify at its expense. Men would follow knowledge and the creation of beauty for their own sakes, and not for the enslavement of their fellows, and they would be rewarded by finding their most necessary work grow interesting and beautiful under their hands without their being conscious of it. The man who felt keenest the pleasure of lying on the hill-side under a rushen hut among the sheep on a summer night, would be no less fit for the enjoyment of the great communal hall with all its splendours of arch and column, and vault and tracery. Nor would he who took to heart the piping of the wind and washing of the waves as he sat at the helm of the fishing-boat, be deadened to the beauty of art-made music. It is workmen only and not pedants who can produce real vigorous art.

And amidst this pleasing labour, and the rest that went with it, would disappear from the earth's face all the traces of the past slavery. Being no longer driven to death by anxiety and fear, we should have time to avoid disgracing the earth with filth and squalor, and accidental ugliness would disappear along with that which was the mere birth of fantastic perversity. The utterly base doctrine, as Carlyle has it, that this world is a cockney nightmare, would be known no more.

But perhaps you may think that Society being thus happy and at peace, its very success would lead it to corruption once more? Yes, that might be if men were not watchful and valiant; but we have begun by saying that they would be free, and free men are bound to be responsible, and that means that they shall be watchful and valiant. The world will be the world still, I do not deny it; but such men as I have been thinking of will surely be fitter to meet its troubles than the dwellers in our present muddle of authority and unconscious revolt.

Or again, some may say such a condition of things might lead indeed to happiness but also to stagnation. Well, to my mind that would be a contradiction in terms, if indeed we agree that happiness is caused by the pleasurable exercise of our faculties. And yet suppose the worst, and that the world did rest after so many troubles—where would be the harm? I remember, after having been ill once, how pleasant it was to lie on my bed without pain or fever, doing nothing but watching the sunbeams and listening to the sounds of life outside; and might not the great world of men, if it once deliver itself from the delirious struggle for life amidst dishonesty, rest for a little after the long fever and be none the worse for it?

Anyhow, I am sure it would be the better for getting rid of its fever, whatever came of it; and sure also that the simplicity of life I have spoken of, which some would call stagnation, would give real life to the great mass of mankind, and to them at least would be a well-spring of happiness. It would raise them at once to a higher level of life, until the world began to be peopled, not with commonplace people, but with honest folk not sharply conscious of their superiority as "intellectual" persons now are, but self-respecting and respecting the personality of others, because they would feel themselves useful and happy, that is alive.

And as for the superior people, if such a world were not good enough for them I am sorry, but am driven to ask them how they manage to get on with the present one, which is worse. I am afraid they would have to answer, We like it better because it *is* worse, and, therefore, relatively we are better.

Alas! my friends, these are the fools who are our masters now. The masters of fools then, you say? Yes, so it is; let us cease to be fools then, and they will be our masters no longer. Believe me, that will be worth trying for, whatever may come afterwards.

Take this for the last word of my dream of what is to be: the test of our being fools no longer will be that we shall no longer have masters.

LONDON IN A STATE OF SIEGE

[Morris described and analysed the events of Bloody Sunday in *Commonweal*, November 19th, 1887. Reprinted in May Morris, II, 251-5.]

SIR Charles Warren has kept his promise and prevented the meeting organized by the Radical Clubs. From the military point of view he had been eminently successful, and deserved to be so, and it is now proper that we should make him a peer of the realm and Commander-in-Chief of the British forces, if he will kindly consent to waive the title of Emperor or three-tailed Bashaw or whatever else is the proper nick-name of a supreme and irresponsible ruler. Sir Charles, I repeat, made his military dispositions admirably, and revolutionists should study them, since they have a little piece of real war suddenly brought to their notice. The "Square," i.e., the sunken space, was guarded by foot-policemen 4 deep, whose business was simply to guard it and who had orders not to stir from their posts, outside these were strong bodies of horse-police who took careful note of any incipient gathering and at once scattered it.

This defence was ample against anything except an organized attack from determined persons acting in concert, and able to depend on one another. In order that no such body should be formed and no such attack be possible, the careful general had posted strong bodies of police, with due supports to fall back on if necessary, about a radius of about a quarter of a mile of the Square, so that nothing could escape falling into the meshes of this net.

Into this net then we marched. The column in which the comrades of the League were, started from Clerkenwell Green in company with the Patriotic Club and some of the

East End clubs, including a Branch of the S.D.F.I see the correspondent of the *Daily News* estimates this column at 6,000, but I think that is an exaggeration. Anyhow, we marched in good order through Theobald's Road, and up Hart Street, crossing Oxford Street and Shaftesbury Avenue without attack from the police, but we had no sooner crossed the latter street and were about to enter the Seven Dials streets to make our way to St Martin's Lane, than the attack came, and it was clearly the best possible place for it. The divergence of the streets would confuse any procession which had lost its rallying point; the side streets and the width of the thoroughfare at the spot gave a good opportunity for a flank charge, and at our rear was the open space of Shaftesbury Avenue to allow a charge in that quarter to finish us up after the attack on front and flank. It was all over in a few minutes: our comrades fought valiantly, but they had not learned how to stand and turn their column into a line, or to march on to the front. Those in front turned and faced their rear, not to run away, but to join in the fray if opportunity served. The police struck right and left like what they were, soldiers attacking an enemy, amid wild shrieks of hatred from the women who came from the slums on our left. The band instruments were captured, the banners and flags destroyed, there was no rallying point and no possibility of rallying, and all that the people composing our once strong column could do was to straggle into the Square as helpless units. I confess I was astounded at the rapidity of the thing and the ease with which military organization got its victory. I could see that numbers were of no avail unless led by a band of men acting in concert and each knowing his own part.

What happened to us happened, as I hear, to the other processions with more or less fighting. An eye-witness who marched up with the western column told me that they were suddenly attacked as they came opposite the Haymarket Theatre, by the police rushing out on them from the side streets and immediately batoning everybody they could reach, whether they resisted or not. The column, he said, was destroyed in two minutes, though certainly not quite without fighting; one brave man wrapping his banner torn from the pole round his arm and facing the police till he was hammered down with repeated blows.

Once in the Square we were, as I said, helpless units, especially as there were undoubtedly a good many mere spectators, many of them club gentlemen and other members of the class which employs Warren. Undoubtedly if two or three hundred men could have been got to make a rush on the cordon of the police, especially at the south-east corner, the crowd could have swarmed into the Square, and if the weakest of the column could have reached the Square in order this could easily have been done. But the result would probably have been a far bloodier massacre than Peterloo; for the people, once in the Square, would have found themselves in a mere penfold at the mercy of the police and soldiers. It is true that as matters went, there seemed very little need for the appearance of the latter, so completely were the police, horse and foot, masters of the situation; and the great mass of the people also round the Square was composed of Radicals, very angry it is true at the horrible brutality with which they had been treated by Warren's men, but by no means strung up to fighting pitch. So that I was fairly surprised, the crowd being then quite quiet, to see the Life Guards form at the south of the Square and march up towards St Martin's Church with the magistrate at their head (a sort of country-gentleman-looking imbecile) to read the Riot Act. The soldiers were cheered as well as hooted by the crowd, I think under the impression that they would not act as brutally against the people as the police: a mistaken impression I think, as these gorgeous gentry are just the helmeted flunkies of the rich and would act on their orders just as their butlers or footmen would do. A little after this a regiment of the foot-guards made their appearance with fixed bayonets, and completed the triumph of law and order.

Sir Charles Warren has thus given us a lesson in street fighting, the first part of which is that mere numbers without organization or drill are useless; the second, which ought also to be noted, is the proper way to defend a position in a large town by a due system of scouts, outposts, and supports.

We Socialists should thank our master for his lesson, and so pass on from considering the military aspect of the case to its civil aspect. Warren has won a victory, but on what terms! It is clear from what is above printed that he would not have been thoroughly successful if he had not had a free hand given him: if he had not attacked citizens marching peaceably through the streets in just such a way as Banditti might do, destroying and stealing their property, they would have been able to claim their right of meeting in Trafalgar Square in such a way that nothing but sharp shot and cold steel could have dealt with them. London has been put under martial law, nominally for behoof of a party, but really on behoof of a class and *war* (for it is no less, whatever the consequences may be) has been forced upon us. The mask is off now, and the real meaning of all the petty persecution of our open-air meetings is as clear as may be. No more humbug need be talked about obstruction and the convenience of the public: it is obvious that those meetings were attacked because we displeased the dominant class and were weak. Last Sunday explains all, and the bourgeois now goes about boasting that he is the master and will do what he likes with his slaves. Again, the humbug is exposed of the political condemnation of coercion by Act of Parliament in Ireland when here in London we have coercion without Act of Parliament; and the feeble twitterings of the *Daily News* will be received with jeers by the triumphant Tories.

And the greatest humbug which Sunday's events have laid bare is "the protection afforded by law to the humblest citizen." Some simple people will be thinking that Warren can be attacked legally for his murderous and cowardly assaults of Sunday. I say Warren, because it is no use beating the *stick* that beats you. Some perhaps will think that there may be a chance of his getting a few years' penal servitude for inciting to riot and murder. But these persons forget that he has been *ordered* to act as he did just as he *ordered* his brigands, and that Salisbury & Co. who *ordered* him have done so at the *orders* of the class which they represent. They have made the laws, but have never intended to keep them when inconvenient. It has now become inconvenient to keep them—and in consequence we must think ourselves lucky to be *only* beaten by the policeman's baton if the bourgeois don't like us—lucky to get off the six months' or twelve months' imprisonment which is likely to accompany such an *accident*. In short, the very Radicals have now been taught that slaves have no rights. The lesson is a painful one, but surely useful to us boastful Englishmen: nay, in the long run it is necessary.

SOCIALISM AND ANARCHISM

[A letter in *Commonweal*, May 5th, 1889. Reprinted in May Morris, II, 312-7.

By this time the Anarchist faction had secured a majority in the Socialist League and the position of Morris was becoming impossible. This letter, a contribution to a discussion then taking place in *Commonweal,* illustrates his firmness in principle but also the courtesy and the comradely spirit with which he conducted a polemic which for him was always a most disagreeable necessity. It shows the falsity of the claims sometimes made that he was really an Anarchist. A little later he remarked in a letter to Bruce Glasier, "in good truth I would almost as soon join a White Rose Society as an Anarchist one; such nonsense as I deem the latter."]

IN answer to our comrade Blackwell's suggestion and in default of someone else beginning that free discussion he speaks of, I wish to note down a few thoughts suggested by reading the clauses of the Anarchist Congress at Valentia, as stated by our comrade; premising that I do so in no polemical spirit, but simply giving my own thoughts and hopes for the future for what they may be worth.

I will begin by saying that I call myself a Communist, and have no wish to qualify that word by joining any other to it. The aim of Communism seems to me to be the complete equality of condition for all people; and anything in a Socialist direction which stops short of this is merely a compromise with the present condition of society, a halting-place on the road to the goal. This is the only logical outcome of any society which is other than a close company sustained by violence for the express purpose of "the exploitation of man by man" in the interest of the strongest. Our present "society" dominated by capitalism, the society of contract, is a form of this class-society which has been forced upon those who hold the slave ideal by the growth of knowledge and the acquirement by man of mastery over the forces of nature. The history of "society" since the fall of feudalism has been the gradual freeing of class or slave-society from the fetters of superstition, so that it might develop naturally within its prescribed limits of "exploitation of man by man," and that stupendous and marvellously rapid growth in power and resources of modern slave-society is due to this shaking off of superstition.

Communism also will have to keep itself free of superstition. Its ethics will have to be based on the recognition of natural cause and effect, and not on rules derived from *a priori* ideas of the relation of man to the universe or some imagined ruler of it; and from these two things, the equality of condition and the recognition of the cause and effect of material nature, will grow all Communistic life. So far I think I can see clearly; but when I try to picture to myself the forms which that life will take, I confess I am at fault, and I think we must all be so. Most people who can be said to think at all are now beginning to see that the realization of Socialism is certain; although many can see no further than a crude and incomplete State Socialism, which very naturally repels many from Socialism altogether. All genuine Socialists admit that Communism is the necessary development of Socialism; but I repeat, further than this all must be speculative; and surely in speculating on the future of society we should try to shake ourselves clear of mere phrases: especially as many of them will cease to have a meaning when the change comes that we all of us long for. And here I join issue with our Anarchist-Communist friends, who are somewhat authoritative on the matter of authority, and not a little vague also. For if freedom from authority means the assertion of the advisability or possibility of an individual man doing what he pleases always and under all circumstances, this is an absolute negation of society, and makes Communism as the highest expression of society impossible; but when you begin to qualify this assertion of the right to do as you please by adding "as long as you don't interfere with other people's rights to do the same," the exercise of some kind of authority becomes necessary. If individuals are not to coerce others, there must somewhere be an authority which is prepared to coerce them not to coerce; and that authority must clearly be collective. And there are other difficulties besides this crudest and most obvious one.

The bond of Communistic society will be voluntary in the sense that all people will agree in its broad principles when it is fairly established, and will trust to it as affording mankind the best kind of life possible. But while we are advocating equality of condition—i.e., due opportunity free to everyone for the satisfaction of his needs—do not let us forget the necessary (and beneficent) variety of temperament, capacity and desires which exists amongst men about everything outside the region of the merest necessaries; and though many, or, if you will, most of these different desires could be satisfied without the individual clashing with collective society, some of them could not be. Any community conceivable will sometimes determine on collective action which, without being in itself immoral or oppressive, would give pain to some of its members; and what is to be done then if it happens to be a piece of business which must be either done or left alone? would the small minority have to give way or the large majority? A concrete example will be of use here, especially as it affects *my* temperament. I have always believed that the realization of Socialism would give us an opportunity of escaping from that grievous flood of utilitarianism which the full development of the society of contract has cursed us with; but that would be in the long run only; and I think it quite probable that in the early days of Socialism the reflex of the terror of starvation, which so oppresses us now, would drive us into excesses of utilitarianism. Indeed, there is a school of Socialists now extant who worship utilitarianism with a fervour of fatuity which is perhaps a natural consequence of their assumption of practicality. So that it is not unlikely that the public opinion of a community would be in favour of cutting down all the timber in England, and turning the country into a big Bonanza farm or a market-garden under glass. And in such a case what could we do? who objected "for the sake of life to cast away the reasons for living," when we had exhausted our powers of argument? Clearly we should have to submit to authority. And a little reflection will show us many such cases in which the collective authority will weigh down individual opposition, however, reasonable, without a hope for its being able to assert itself immediately; in such matters there must be give and take: and the objectors would have to give up the lesser for the greater. In short, experience shows us that wherever a dozen thoughtful men shall meet together there will be twelve different opinions on any subject which is not a dry matter of fact (and often on that too); and if those twelve men want to act together, there must be give and take between them, and they must agree on some common rule of conduct to act as a bond between them, or leave their business undone. And what is this common bond but authority—that is, the conscience of the association voluntarily accepted in the first instance.

Furthermore, when we talk of the freedom of the individual man, we must not forget that every man is a very complex animal, made up of many different moods and impulses; no man is always wise, or wise in all respects. Philip sober needs protection against Philip drunk, or he may chance to wake up from his booze in a nice mess. Surely we all of us feel that there is a rascal or two in each of our skins besides the other or two who want to lead manly and honourable lives, and do we not want something to appeal to on behalf of those better selves of ours? and that something is made up of the aspirations of our better selves, and is the *social conscience* without which there can be no true society, and which even a false society is forced to imitate, and so have a sham social conscience—what we sometimes call hypocrisy.

Now I don't want to be misunderstood. I am not pleading for any form of arbitrary or unreasonable authority, but for a *public conscience* as a rule of action: and by all means let us have the least possible exercise of authority. I suspect that many of our Communist-Anarchist friends do really mean that, when they pronounce against all authority. And with equality of condition assured for all men, and our ethics based on reason, I cannot think that we need fear the growth of a new authority taking the place of the one which we should have destroyed, and which we must remember is based on the assumption that equality is impossible and that slavery is an essential condition of human society. By the time it is assumed that all men's needs must be satisfied according [to] the measure of the common wealth, what may be called the political side of the question would take care of itself.

UNDER AN ELM-TREE;
OR THOUGHTS IN THE COUNTRY-SIDE

[Published in *Commonweal*, July 6th, 1889. May Morris, II, 507-12.

At the height of his difficulties with the Anarchists Morris was still able to express a serene confidence in the ultimate triumph of Socialism. The White Horse is a gigantic figure cut in the turf of the Berkshire Downs at Uffington. Now attributed to the late Iron Age it was then thought to commemorate Alfred's victory over the Danes at Ashdown in 871. Periodically it was cleaned and re-cut at a kind of folk festival accompanied by feasting and traditional games. The last such occasion, in 1854, was described by Thomas Hughes in the *Scouring of the White Horse,* a delightful book with which Morris must have been familiar.]

MIDSUMMER in the country: here you may walk between the fields and hedges that are as it were one huge nosegay for you, redolent of bean-flowers and clover and sweet hay and elder-blossom. The cottage-gardens are bright with flowers, the cottages themselves mostly models of architecture in their way. Above them towers here and there the architecture proper of days bygone, when every craftsman was an artist and brought definite intelligence to bear upon his work. Man in the past, nature in the present, seem to be bent on pleasing you and making all things delightful to your senses; even the burning dusty road has a look of luxury as you lie on the strip of roadside green, and listen to the blackbirds singing, surely for your benefit, and, I was going to say, as if they were paid to do it, but I was wrong, for as it is they seem to be doing their best.

And all, or let us say most, things are brilliantly alive.

The shadowy bleak in the river down yonder, which—ignorant of the fate that Barking Reach is preparing for its waters—is sapphire blue under this ruffling wind and cloudless sky, and barred across here and there with the pearly white-flowered water-weeds, every yard of its banks a treasure of delicate design, meadowsweet and dewberry, and comfrey and bed-straw: from the bleak in the river, among the labyrinth of grasses, to the starlings busy in the new-shorn fields, or about the grey ridges of the hay, all is eager, and I think all is happy that is not anxious.

What is that thought that has come into one's head as one turns round in the shadow of the roadside elm? A country-side worth fighting for, if that were necessary, worth taking trouble to defend its peace. I raise my head, and betwixt the elm-boughs I see far off a grey buttressed down rising over the sea of green and blue-green meadows and fields, and dim on the flank of it over its buttresses I can see a quaint figure made by cutting the short turf away from the chalk of the hill-side; a figure which represents a White Horse according to the heraldry of the period, eleven hundred years ago. Hard by the hillside the country people of the day did verily fight for the peace and loveliness of this very country where I lie, and coming back from their victory scored the image of the White Horse as a token of their valour, and, who knows? perhaps as an example for their descendants to follow.

For a little time it makes the blood stir in me as I think of that; but as I watch the swallows flitting past me betwixt hedge and hedge, or mounting over the hedge in an easy sweep and hawking over the bean-field beyond, another thought comes over me. These live things I have been speaking of, bleak and swallows and starlings and blackbirds, are all after their kind beautiful and graceful, not one of them is lacking in its due grace and beauty; but yesterday as I was passing by a hay-field there was an old red-roan cart-horse looking seriously but good-humouredly at me from a gap in the hedge, and I stopped to make his acquaintance, and I am sorry to say that in spite of his obvious merits he was ugly, Roman-nosed, shambling, ungainly; yet how useful had he been—for others. Also the same day (but not in the same field) I saw some other animals, male and female, with whom also I made aquaintance, for the male ones at least were thirsty. And these animals, both male and female, were ungraceful, unbeautiful, for they were making hay before my eyes. Then I bethought me that as I had seen starlings in Hertfordshire that were of the same race as the Thames-side starlings, so I had seen or heard of featherless, two-legged animals of the same race as the thirsty creatures in the hay-field; they had been sculptured in the frieze of the Parthenon, painted on the ceiling of the Sistine Chapel, imagined in literature as the heroes and heroines of romance; nay, when people had created in their minds a god of the universe, creator of all that was, is, or shall be, they were driven to represent him as one of that same race to which the thirsty haymakers belonged; as though supreme intelligence and the greatest measure of gracefulness and beauty and majesty were at their highest in the race of those ungainly animals.

Under the elm-tree these things puzzle me, and again my thoughts return to the bold men of that very country-side who, coming back from Ashdown field, scored that White Horse to look down for ever on the valley of the Thames; and I thought it likely that they had this much in common with the starlings and the bleak, that there was more equality among them than we are used to now, and that there would have been more models available amongst them for Woden than one would be like to find in the Thames-side meadows.

Under the elm-tree I don't ask myself whether that is owing to the greater average intelligence of men at the present day, and to the progress of humanity made since the time of the only decent official that England ever had; Alfred the Great, to wit; for indeed the place and time are not favourable to such questions, which seem sheer nonsense amidst of all that waste of superabundant beauty and pleasure held out to men who cannot take it or use it, unless some chance rich idler may happen to stray that way. My thoughts turn back to the haymakers and their hopes, and I remember that yesterday morning I said to a by-stander, "Mr So-and-so (the farmer) is late in sending his men into the hayfield."

Quoth he, "You see, sir, Mr So-and-so is short-handed."

"How's that?" said I, pricking up my Socialist ears.

"Well, sir," said he, "these men are the old men and women bred in the village, and pretty much past work; and the young men with more work in them, they do think that they ought to have more wages than them, and Mr So-and-so he won't pay it. So you see, he be short-handed."

As I turned away, thinking over all the untold, untellable details of misery that lay within this shabby sordid story, another one met my ears. A labourer of the village comes to a farmer and says to him that he really can't work for 9s. a week any more, but must have 10s. Says the farmer, "Get your 10s. somewhere else then." The man turns away to two months' lack of employment, and then comes back begging for his 9s. slavery.

Commonplace stories of unsupported strikes, you will say. Indeed they are, if not they would be easily remedied; the casual tragedy cut short; the casual wrong-doer branded as a person out of humanity. But since they are so com-monplace—

What will happen, say my gloomy thoughts to me under the elm-tree, with all this country beauty so tragically in-congruous in its richness with the country misery which cannot feel its existence? Well, if we must still be slaves and slave-holders, it will not last long: the Battle of Ash-down will be forgotten for the last commercial crisis: Alfred's heraldry will yield to the lions on the half crown. The architecture of the crafts-gildsmen will tumble down, or be "restored" for the benefit of hunters of the picturesque, who, hopeless themselves, are incapable of understand-ing the hopes of past days, or the expression of them. The beauty of the landscape will be exploited and artificialized for the sake of villa-dwellers' purses where it is striking enough to touch their jaded appetites; but in quiet places like this it will vanish year by year (as indeed it is now doing) under the attacks of the most grovelling commercialism.

Yet think I to myself under the elm-tree, whatever England, once so beautiful, may become, it will be good enough for us if we set no hope before us but the continuance of a population of slaves and slave-holders for the country which we pretend to love, while we use it and our sham love for it as a stalking-horse for robbery of the poor at home and abroad. The worst outward ugliness and vulgarity will be good enough for such sneaks and cowards.

Let me turn the leaf and find a new picture, or my holiday is spoilt; and don't let some of my Socialist friends with whom I have wrangled about the horrors of London say, "This is all that can come of your country life." For as the round of the seasons under our system of landlord, farmer and labourer produces in the country pinching parsimony and dulness, so does the "excitement of intellectual life" in the cities produce the slum under the capitalist system of turning out and selling market wares not for use but for waste. Turn the page, I say. The hayfield is a pretty sight this month seen under the elm, as the work goes forward on the other side of the way opposite to the beanfield, till you look at the haymakers closely. Suppose the haymakers were friends working for friends on land which was theirs, as many as were needed, with leisure and hope ahead of them instead of hopeless toil and anxiety, need their useful labour for themselves and their neighbours cripple and disfigure them and knock them out of the shape of men fit to represent the Gods and Heroes? If under such conditions a new Ashdown had to be fought (against *capitalist* robbers this time), the new White Horse would look down on the home of men as wise as the starlings, in their *equality,* and so perhaps as happy.

WHERE ARE WE NOW?

[Published in *Commonweal*, November 15th, 1890. May Morris, II, 512-8.

This is Morris' farewell to the Socialist League, now in a state of complete disintegration. He takes the opportunity to review the progress of Socialism since he joined the Democratic Federation in 1883. At the same time it illustrates one of his main weaknesses, his inability to see how to combine the struggle for Socialism with the struggle for immediate demands—a weakness very common among the Socialists of his time.]

IT is good from time to time for those who are engaged in a serious movement to look back and review the progress of the past few years; which involves looking around them and noting the way the movement is affecting other people. It is good to do so for this reason amongst others, that men absorbed in such a movement are apt to surround themselves with a kind of artificial atmosphere which distorts the proportions of things outside, and prevents them from seeing what is really going on, and consequently from taking due counsel as to what is best to do.

It is now some seven years since Socialism came to life again in this country. To some the time will seem long, so many hopes and disappointments as have been crowded into them. Yet in the history of a serious movement seven years is a short time enough; and few movements surely have made so much progress during this short time in one way or another as Socialism has done.

For what was it which we set out to accomplish? To change the system of society on which the stupendous fabric of civilization is founded, and which has been built up by centuries of conflict with older and dying systems, and crowned by the victory of modern civilization over the material surroundings of life.

Could seven years make any visible impression on such a tremendous undertaking as this?

Consider, too, the quality of those who began and carried on this business of reversing the basis of modern society. Who were the statesmen who took up the momentous questions laid before England of the nineteenth century by the English Socialists? Who were the great divines who preached this new gospel of happiness from their pulpits? Who were the natural philosophers who proclaimed their hope and joy at the advent of a society which should at last use their marvellous discoveries for the good of mankind?

There is no need to take a pen in hand to write their names. The traveller (i.e., the toiler) had fallen among thieves, and the priest and the Levite went by on the other side; or perhaps in this case threw a stone or two at the wounded man: it was but a Samaritan, an outcast, an unrespectable person, who helped him.

Those who set out "to make the revolution"—that is, as aforesaid, to put society on a new basis, contradictory to the existing one—were a few working men, less successful even in the wretched life of labour than their fellows; a sprinkling of the intellectual proletariat, whose keen pushing of Socialism must have seemed pretty certain to extinguish their limited chances of prosperity; one or two outsiders in the game political; a few refugees from the bureaucratic tyranny of foreign governments; and here and there an unpractical, half-cracked artist or author.

Yet such as they were, they were enough to do something. Through them, though not by them, the seven years of the new movement toward freedom have, contrary to all that might have been expected, impressed the idea of Socialism deeply on the epoch. It is true that the toilers have not begun to reap benefit from that impression; but it was impossible that they should. No permanent material benefit *can* accrue to them until Socialism has ceased to be militant, and is merged in the new society. But as I said the other week, the movement has at least accomplished this, that no one who thinks is otherwise than discontented with things as they are. The shouts of triumph over the glories of civilization which once drowned the moans of the miserable (and that but a dozen years ago at most) have now sunk into quavering apologies for the existence of the horrors and fatuities of our system; a system which is only defended as a thing to be endured for lack of a better, and until we can find some means of packing it off into limbo; and the workers, who in the period of "leap and bound prosperity" were thought to have reached the end of their tether, and to be fixed in a kind of subordinate heaven on earth, are now showing that they are not going to stop *there,* at any rate, and whatever happens. And the principles of Socialism are beginning to be understood, so that to some of ourselves, who are always hearing of them, they seem now mere commonplaces which need not be insisted on. Though with that view I can, as I shall show presently, by no means agree.

All this has come to pass. How and why? Was it by virtue of the qualities of those who have furthered it? That little band of oddities who fell in with Socialism during these last few years, did it turn out after all that they were so much better than they seemed? Well, they were (and are), most of them, human at least; but otherwise it cannot be said that great unexpected talent for administration and conduct of affairs has been developed amongst us, nor any vast amount of foresight either. We have been what we seemed to be (to our friends I hope)—and that was no great thing. We have between us made about as many mistakes as any other party in a similar space of time. Quarrels more than enough we have had; and sometimes also weak assent for fear of quarrels to what we did not agree with.

There has been self-seeking amongst us, and vainglory, and sloth, and rashness; though there has been at least courage and devotion also. When I first joined the move-ment I hoped that some working-man leader, or rather leaders, would turn up, who would push aside all middle-class help, and become great historical figures. I might still hope for that, if it seemed likely to happen, for indeed I long for it enough; but to speak plainly it does not so seem at present.

Yet, I repeat, in spite of all drawbacks the impression has been made, and why? The reason for it has been given in words said before, but which I must needs say again: because that seemingly inexpugnable fabric of modern society is verging towards its fall; it has done its work, and is going to change into something else. That is the reason why, with all our faults, we have been able to do something; nor do I believe that there will ever be lacking instruments for bringing about the great change, exactly in proportion to the readiness of the solid elements in society—the workers, to wit—to receive that change, and carry on the new order to which it will give birth.

So much at least we have to encourage us. But are not some of us disappointed in spite of the change of the way in which Socialism is looked on generally? It is but natural that we should be. When we first began to work together, there was little said about anything save the great ideals of Socialism; and so far off did we seem from the realiza-tion of these, that we could hardly think of any means for their realization, save great dramatic events which would make our lives tragic indeed, but would take us out of the sordidness of the so-called "peace" of civilization. With the great extension of Socialism, this also is changed. Our very success has dimmed the great ideals that first led us on; for the hope of the partial and, so to say, vulgarized realization of Socialism is now pressing on us. I think that we are all confident that Socialism will be realized: it is not wonderful, then, that we should long to see, to feel, its realization in our own life-time. Methods of realization, therefore, are now more before our eyes than ideals: but it is of no use talking about methods which are not, in part at least, immediately feasible, and it is of the nature of such partial methods to be sordid and discouraging, though they *may* be necessary.

There are two tendencies in this matter of methods: on the one hand is our old acquaintance palliation, elevated now into vastly greater importance than it used to have, because of the growing discontent, and the obvious advance of Socialism; on the other is the method of partial, necessarily futile, inconsequent revolt, or riot rather, against the authorities, who are our absolute masters, and can easily put it down.

With both of these methods I disagree; and that the more because the palliatives have to be clamoured for, and the riots carried out by men who do not know what Socialism is, and have no idea what their next step is to be, if contrary to all calculation they should happen to be successful. Therefore, at the best our masters would be our masters still, because there would be nothing to take their place. *We are not ready for such a change as that!* The authorities might be a little shaken perhaps, a little more inclined to yield something to the clamours of their slaves, but there would be slaves still, *as all men must be who are not prepared to manage their own business themselves.* Nay, as to the partial violent means, I believe that the occurrence of these would not shake the authorities at all, but would strengthen them rather, because they would draw to them the timid of all classes, i.e., all men but a very few.

I have mentioned the two lines in which what I should call the methods of impatience profess to work. Before I write a very few words on the only line of method on which some of us *can* work, I will give my views about the present state of the movement as briefly as I can.

The whole set opinion amongst those more or less touched by Socialism, who are not definite Socialists, is towards the New Trades Unionism and palliation. Men believe that they can wrest from the capitalists some portion of their privileged profits, and the masters, to judge by the recent threats of combination on their side, believe also that this can be done. That it could only very partially be done, and that the men could not rest there if it were done, we Socialists know very well; but others do not. Let that pass for the present. The Parliamentary side of things seems in abeyance, at present; it has given place to the Trade Union side. But, of course, it will come up again; and in time, if there is nothing to cut across the logical sequence of events, it will achieve the *legal* Eight Hours' Day—with next to no results either to men or masters.

For the rest, I neither believe in State Socialism as desirable in itself, or, indeed, as a complete scheme do I think it possible. Nevertheless, some approach to it is sure to be tried, and to my mind this will precede any complete enlightenment on the new order of things. The success of Mr Bellamy's Utopian book, deadly dull as it is, is a straw to show which way the wind blows. The general attention paid to our clever friends, the Fabian lecturers and pamphleteers, is not altogether due to their literary ability; people have really got their heads turned more or less in their direction.

Now it seems to me that at such a time, when people are not only discontented, but have really conceived a hope of bettering the condition of labour, while at the same time the means towards their end are doubtful: or, rather, when they take the very beginning of the means as an end in itself: that this time when people are excited about Socialism, and when many who know nothing about it think themselves Socialists, is the time of all others to put forward the simple principles of Socialism regardless of the policy of the passing hour.

My readers will understand· that in saying this I am speaking for those who are complete Socialists, or let us call them Communists. I say for us *to make Socialists* is *the* business at present, and at present I do not think we can have any other useful business. Those who are not really Socialists—who are Trades Unionists, disturbance-breeders, or what not—will do what they are impelled to do, and we cannot help it. At the worst there will be some good in what they do; but we need not and cannot heartily work with them, when we know that their methods are beside the right way.

Our business, I repeat, is the making of Socialists, i.e., convincing people that Socialism is good for them and is possible. When we have enough people of that way of thinking, *they* will find out what action is necessary for putting their principles in practice. Until we have that mass of opinion, action for a general change that will benefit the whole people is *impossible.* Have we that body of opinion or anything like it? Surely not. If we look outside that glamour, that charmed atmosphere of party warfare in which we necessarily move, we shall see this clearly: that though there are a great many who believe it possible to compel their masters by some means or another to behave better to them, and though they are prepared to compel them (by so-called peaceful means, strikes and the like), all but a very small minority are not prepared *to do without masters.* They do not believe in their own capacity to undertake the management of affairs, and to be responsible for their life in this world. When they are so prepared, then Socialism will be realized; but nothing can push it on a day in advance of that time.

Therefore, I say, make Socialists. We Socialists can do nothing else that is useful, and preaching and teaching is not out of date for that purpose; but rather for those who, like myself, do not believe in State Socialism, it is the only rational means of attaining to the New Order of Things.

COMMUNISM

[A lecture delivered to the Hammersmith Socialist Society at Kelmscott House on March 10th, 1893. First published as a Fabian tract, 1903. *Collected Works*, XXIII, 264-76, Cole, 660-76, Jackson, 325-33.

In this lecture Morris re-thinks his Socialism in the light of new developments, but there is no weakening of his revolutionary conviction.]

WHILE I think that the hope of the new-birth of society is certainly growing, and that speedily, I must confess myself puzzled about the means toward that end which are mostly looked after now; and I am doubtful if some of the measures which are pressed, mostly, I think, with all honesty of purpose, and often with much ability, would, if gained, bring us any further on the direct road to a really new-born society, the only society which can be a new birth, a society of practical equality. Not to make any mystery about it, I mean that the great mass of what most non-socialists at least consider at present to be socialism, seems to me nothing more than a *machinery* of socialism, which I think it probable that socialism *must* use in its militant condition; and which I think it *may* use for some time after it is practically established; but does not seem to me to be of its essence. Doubtless there is good in the schemes for substituting business-like administration in the interests of the public for the old Whig muddle of *laissez-faire* backed up by coercion and smoothed by abundant corruption, which, worked all of it in the interest of successful business men, was once thought such a wonderful invention, and which certainly was the very cement of society as it has existed since the death of feudalism. The London County Council, for instance, is not merely a more useful body for the administration of public business than the Metropolitan Board of Works was: it is instinct with a different spirit; and even its general *intention* to be of use to the citizens and to heed their wishes, has in it a promise of better days, and has already done something to raise the dignity of life in London amongst a certain part of the population, and down to certain classes. Again, who can quarrel with the attempts to relieve the sordidness of civilized town life by the public acquirement of parks and other open spaces, planting of trees, establishment of free libraries and the like? It is sensible and right for the public to push for the attainment of such gains; but we all know very well that their advantages are very unequally distributed, that they are gains rather for certain portions of the middle classes than for working people. Nay, this socialist machinery may be used much further: it may gain higher wages and shorter working hours for the working men themselves: industries may be worked by municipalities for the benefit both of producers and consumers. Working-people's houses may be improved, and their management taken out of the hands of commercial speculators. More time might be insisted on for the education of children; and so on, and so on. In all this I freely admit a great gain, and am glad to see schemes tried which would lead to it. But great as the gain would be, the ultimate good of it, the amount of progressive force that might be in such things would, I think, depend on *how* such reforms were done; in what spirit; or rather what else was being done, while these were going on, which would make people long for equality of condition; which would give them faith in the possibility and workableness of socialism; which would give them courage to strive for it and labour for it; and which would do this for a vast number of people, so that the due impetus might be gained for the sweeping away of all privilege. For we must not lose sight of the very obvious fact that these improvements in the life of the larger public can only be carried out at the expense of some portion of the freedom and fortunes of the proprietary classes. They are, when genuine, one and all attacks I say on the "liberty and property" of the non-working or useless classes, as some of those classes see clearly enough. And I admit that if the sum of them should become vast and deep reaching enough to give to the useful or working-classes intelligence enough to conceive of a life of equality and co-operation; courage enough to accept it and to bring the necessary skill to bear on working it; and power enough to force its acceptance on the stupid and the interested, the war of classes would speedily end in the victory of the useful class, which would then become the new society of Equality.

Intelligence enough to conceive, courage enough to will, power enough to compel. If our ideas of a new Society are anything more than a dream, these three qualities must animate the due effective majority of the working people; and then, I say, the thing will be done.

Intelligence, courage, power *enough*. Now that *enough* means a very great thing. The effective majority of the working people must I should think be something as great in numbers as an actual mechanical majority; because the non-working classes (with, mind you, their sworn slaves and parasites, men who can't live without them) are even numerically very strong, and are stronger still in holding in their hand the nine points of the law, possession to wit; and as soon as these begin to think there is any serious danger to their privilege—i.e., their livelihood—they will be pretty much unanimous in defending it, and using all the power which they possess in doing so. The necessary majority therefore of intelligence, courage, and power is such a big thing to bring about, that it will take a long time to do so; and those who are working for this end must clearly not throw away time and strength by making more mistakes than they can possibly help in their efforts for the conversion of the working people to an ardent desire for a society of equality. The question then, it seems to me, about all those partial gains above mentioned, is not so much as to what advantage they may be to the public at large in the passing moment, or even to the working people, but rather what effect they will have towards converting the workers to an understanding of, and ardent desire for Socialism; true and complete Socialism I mean, what I should call Communism. For though making a great many poor people, or even a few, somewhat more comfortable than they are now, somewhat less miserable, let us say, is not in itself a light good; yet it would be a heavy evil, if it did anything towards dulling the efforts of the whole class of workers towards the winning of a real society of equals. And here again come in those doubts and the puzzlement I began by talking about. For I want to know and to ask you to consider, how far the betterment of the working people might go and yet stop at last without having made any progress on the *direct* road to Communism. Whether in short the tremendous organization of civilized commercial society is not playing the cat and mouse game with us socialists. Whether the Society of Inequality might not accept the quasi-socialist machinery above mentioned, and work it for the purpose of upholding that society in a somewhat shorn condition, maybe, but a safe one. That seems to me possible, and means the other side of the view: instead of the useless classes being swept away by the useful, the useless classes gaining some of the usefulness of the workers, and *so* safeguarding their privilege. The workers better treated, better organized, helping to govern themselves, but with no more pretence to equality with the rich, nor any more hope for it than they have now. But if this be possible, it will only be so on the grounds that the working people have ceased to desire real socialism and are contented with some outside show of it joined to an increase in prosperity enough to satisfy the cravings of men who do not know what the pleasures of life might be if they treated their own capacities and the resources of nature reasonably with the intention and expectation

of being happy. Of course also it could not be possible if
there be, as we may well hope, an actual necessity for
new development of society from out of our present
conditions: but granting this necessity, the change may
and will be exceedingly slow in coming if the working
people do not show their sense of the necessity by being
overtaken by a longing for the change and by expressing
that longing. And moreover it will not only be slow in
coming but also in that case it can only come through a
period of great suffering and misery, by the ruin of our
present civilization: and surely reasonable men must
hope that if the Socialism be necessary its advent shall
both be speedy and shall be marked by the minimum of
suffering and by ruin not quite complete. Therefore, I
say, what we have to hope for is that the inevitable
advance of the society of equality will speedily make itself
felt by the consciousness of its necessity being impressed
upon the working people, and that they will consciously
and not blindly strive for its realization. That in fact is
what we mean by the education into Socialism of the
working classes. And I believe that if this is impossible
at present, if the working people refuse to take any
interest in Socialism, if they practically reject it, we must
accept that as a sign that the necessity for an essential
change in society is so far distant, that we need scarcely
trouble ourselves about it. This is the test; and for this
reason it is so deadly serious for us to find out whether
those democratic tendencies and the schemes of new
administration they give birth to are really of use in
educating the people into *direct* Socialism. If they are not,
they are of use for nothing else; and we had best try if
we can't make terms with intelligent Tories and benevolent Whigs, and beg them to unite their intelligence and
benevolence, and govern us as kindly and wisely as they
can, and to rob us in moderation only. But if they are
of use, then in spite of their sordid and repellent details,
and all the sickness of hope deferred that the use of such
instruments assuredly brings us, let us use them as far

as they will go, and refuse to be disappointed if they will
not go very far: which means if they will not in a decade
turn into a united host of heroes and sages a huge mass of
men living under a system of society so intricate as to look
on the surface like a mere chance-hap muddle of many
millions of necessitous people, oppressed indeed, and
sorely, not by obvious individual violence and ill-will,
but by an economic system so far reaching, so deeply
seated, that it may well seem like the operation of a
natural law to men so uneducated that they have not even
escaped the reflexion of the so-called education of their
masters, but in addition to their other mishaps are
saddled also with the superstitions and hypocrisies of the
upper classes, with scarce a whit of the characteristic
traditions of their own class to help them: an intellectual
slavery which is a necessary accompaniment of their
material slavery. That as a mass is what revolutionists
have got to deal with; such a mass indeed I think could
and would be vivified by some spark of enthusiasm,
some sudden hopeful impulse towards aggression, if the
necessity for sudden change were close at hand. But is it?
There are doubtless not a few in this room, myself
perhaps amongst them (I say *perhaps* for one's old self is
apt to grow dim to one)—some of us I say once believed
in the inevitableness of a sudden and speedy change. That
was no wonder with the new enlightenment of socialism
gilding the dullness of civilization for us. But if we must
now take soberer views of our hopes, do not reproach us
with that. Remember how hard other tyrannies have died,
though to the economical oppression of them was added
obvious violent individual oppression, which as I have
said is lacking to the heavy tyranny of our times; and can
we hope that it will be speedier in its ending than they? I
say that the time is not now for the sudden kindling of the
impulse of direct aggression amongst the mass of the
workmen. But what then; are we to give up all hope of
educating them into Socialism? Surely not. Let us use all
means possible for drawing them into socialism, so that

they may at last find themselves in such a position that they understand themselves to be face to face with false society, themselves the only possible elements of true society.

So now I must say that I am driven to the conclusion that those measures I have been speaking of, like everything that under any reasonable form does tend towards socialism (present conditions being understood) *are* of use toward the education of the great mass of the workers; that it is necessary in the present to give form to vague aspirations which are in the air about them, and to raise their aims above the mere businesslike work of the old trades unions of raising wages with the consent (however obtained) of the employers; of making the workers see other employers[1] than those who live on the profit wrung out of their labour. I think that taking up such measures, directly tending towards Socialism, is necessary also in getting working people to raise their standard of livelihood so that they may claim more and yet more of the wealth produced by society, which as aforesaid they can only get at the expense of the non-producing classes who now rob them. Lastly, such measures, with all that goes towards getting them carried, will train them into organization and administration; and I hope that no one here will assert that they do not need such training, or that they are not at a huge disadvantage from the lack of it as compared with their masters who have been trained in these arts.

But this education by political and corporate action must, as I hinted above, be supplemented by instilling into the minds of the people a knowledge of the aims of socialism, and a longing to bring about the complete change which will supplant civilization by communism. For the Social-democratic measures above mentioned are all of them either makeshift alleviations to help us through the present

---

1 The public to wit, i.e., the workers themselves in their other position of consumers.

days of oppression, or means for landing us in the new country of equality. And there is a danger that they will be looked upon as ends in themselves. Nay it is certain that the greater number of those who are pushing for them will at the time be able to see no further than them, and will only recognize their temporary character when they have passed beyond them, and are claiming the next thing. But I must hope that we can instil into the mass of people some spirit of expectation, however vague, beyond the needs of the year; and I know that many who are on the road to socialism will from the first and habitually look toward the realization of the society of equality, and try to realize it for themselves—I mean they will at least try to think what equality will turn out to be, and will long for it above all things. And I look to this spirit to vivify the striving for the mere machinery of Socialism; and I hope and believe that it will so spread as the machinery is attained that however much the old individualist spirit may try to make itself master of the corporate machinery, and try by means of the public to govern the public in the interests of the enemies of the public, it may be defeated.

All this however is talking about the possible course of the Socialist movement; but since, as you have just heard, it seems to me necessary that in order to make any due use of socialist machinery one should have some sort of idea as to the life which is to be the result of it, let me now take up the often told tale of what we mean by communism or socialism; for between complete Socialism and Communism there is no difference whatever in my mind. Communism is in fact the completion of Socialism: when that ceases to be militant and becomes triumphant, it will be communism.

The Communist asserts in the first place that the resources of nature, mainly the land and those other things which can only be used for the reproduction of wealth and which are the effect of social work, should not be owned in severalty, but by the whole community for the benefit of the whole. That where this is not the case the owners of these means of production must of necessity be the masters of those who do not own a sufficiency of them to free them from the need of paying with a portion of their labour for the use of the said means of production; and that the masters or owners of the means of production do practically own the workers; very practically, since they really dictate to them the kind of life they shall lead, and the workers cannot escape from it unless by themselves becoming owners of the means of production, i.e. of other men. The resources of nature therefore, and the wealth used for the production of further wealth, the plant and stock in short, should be communized. Now if that were done, it would at once check the accumulation of riches. No man can become immensely rich by the storing up of wealth which is the result of the labour of his own brain and hands: to become very rich he must by cajolery or force deprive others of what their brains or hands have earned for them: the utmost that the most acquisitive man could do would be to induce his fellow-citizens to pay him extra for his special talents, if they specially longed for his productions. But since no one could be very rich, and since talent for special work is never so very rare, and would tend to become less rare as men were freer to choose the occupations most suitable for them, producers of specialities could not exact *very* exorbitant payment, so that the aristocracy of talent even if it appeared, would tend to disappear, even in this first state of incomplete Communism. In short there would be no very rich men: and all would be well off: all would be far above the condition of satisfaction to their material necessities. You may say how do I know that? The answer is because there could not be so much waste as there is now. Waste would tend to disappear. For what is waste? First, the causeless destruction of raw material; and secondly, the diverting of labour from useful production. You may ask me what is the standard of usefulness in wares? It has been said, and I suppose the common view of that point is, that the price in the market gives us the standard; but is a loaf of bread or a saw less useful than a Mechlin lace veil or a diamond necklace? The truth is that in a society of inequality, a society in which there are very rich people and very poor ones, the standard of usefulness is utterly confused: in such a society the market price of an article is given us by the necessities of the poor and the inordinate cravings of the rich; or rather indeed *their* necessity for spending their wealth—or rather their riches—somehow: by no means necessarily in pleasure. But in a society of equality the demand for an article *would* be a standard of its usefulness in one way or other. And it would be a matter of course that until everybody had his absolute necessities and his reasonable comforts satisfied, there would be no place for the production of luxuries; and always labour would be employed in producing things that people (all the people, since classes would have disappeared) really want.

Remember what the waste of a society of inequality is: 1st: The production of sordid makeshifts for the supply of poor folk who cannot afford the real article. 2nd: the production of luxuries for rich folk, the greater part of which even their personal folly does not make them want. And 3rdly: the wealth wasted by the salesmanship of competitive commerce, to which the production of wares is but a secondary object, its first object being the production of a profit for the individual manufacturer. You understand that the necessary distribution of goods is not included in this waste; but the endeavour of each manufacturer to get as near as he can to a monopoly of the market which he supplies.

The minimization of waste therefore, which would take place in the incomplete 1st stages of a society of equality—a society only *tending* to equality—would make us wealthy: labour would not be wasted: workmen would not be employed in producing either slave wares, or toys for rich men: their genuine well made wares would be made for other workmen who would know what they wanted. When the wares were of such a kind as required very exquisite skill and long training to produce, or when the material used was far fetched and dear bought, they would not cease to be produced, even though private citizens could not acquire them: they would be produced for the public use, and their real value be enormously increased thereby, and the natural and honest pride of the workman duly satisfied. For surely wealthy people will not put up with sordid surroundings or stinginess in public institutions: they will assuredly have schools, libraries, museums, parks and all the rest of it real and genuine, not makeshifts for such things; especially as being no longer oppressed by fears for their livelihood, and all the dismal incidents of the battle for mere existence, they will be able to enjoy these things thoroughly: they will be able in fact to use them, which they cannot do now. But in all I have been saying about this new society hitherto I have been thinking I must remind you of its inchoate and incomplete stages. The means of production communized but the resulting wealth still private property. Truth to tell, I think that such a state of things could only embrace a very short period of transition to complete communism: a period which would only last while people were shaking down into the new Society; for if there were no poor people I don't see how there could be any rich. There would indeed be a natural compulsion, which would prevent any man from doing what he was not fitted for, because he could not do it usefully; and I need not say that in order to arrive at the wealth I have been speaking of we must all work usefully. But if a man does work usefully you can't do without him; and if you can't do without him you can only put him into an inferior position to another useful citizen by means of compulsion; and if you compel him to it, you at once have your privileged classes again. Again, when all people are living comfortably or even handsomely, the keenness of the strife for the better positions, which will then no longer involve a life of idleness or power over one's neighbours, will surely tend to abate: men get rich now in their struggles not to be poor, and because their riches shield them from suffering from the horrors which are a necessary accompaniment of the existence of rich men; e.g., the sight of slums, the squalor of a factory country, the yells and evil language of drunken and brutalized poor people and so forth. But when all private life was decent and, apart from natural accident, happy; and when public institutions satisfied your craving for splendour and completeness; and when no one was allowed to injure the public by defiling the natural beauty of the earth, or by forbidding men's cravings for making it more beautiful to have full sway, what advantage would there be in having more nominal wealth than your neighbour? Therefore, as on the one hand men whose work was acknowledged as useful would scarcely subject themselves to a new system of caste; and, on the other, people living happily with all their reasonable needs easily satisfied would hardly worry themselves with worrying others into giving them extra wealth which they could not use, so I think the communization of the means of industry would speedily be followed by the communization of its product: that is that there would be complete equality of condition amongst all men. Which again does not mean that people would (all round) use their neighbours' coats, or houses or tooth brushes, but that every one, whatever work he did, would have the opportunity of satisfying all his reasonable needs according to the admitted standard of the society in which he lived: i.e., without robbing any other citizen. And I must say it is in the belief that this is possible of realization that I continue to be a socialist. Prove to me that it is not; and I will not trouble myself to do my share towards altering the present state of society, but will try to live on, as little a pain to myself and a nuisance to my neighbour as I may. But yet I must tell that I shall be more or less both a pain to myself (or at least a disgrace) and a nuisance to my neighbour. For I do declare that any other state of society but communism is grievous and disgraceful to all belonging to it.

Some of you may expect me to say something about the machinery by which a communistic society is to be carried on. Well, I can say very little that is not merely negative.

Most anti-socialists and even some socialists are apt to confuse, as I hinted before, the co-operative machinery towards which modern life is tending with the essence of socialism itself; and its enemies attack it, and sometimes its friends defend it on those lines; both to my mind committing a grievous error, especially the latter. E.g. An anti-socialist will say How will you sail a ship in a socialist condition? How? Why with a captain and mates and sailing master and engineer (if it be a steamer) and ABs and stokers and so on and so on. *Only* there will be no 1st, 2nd and 3rd class among the passengers: the sailors and stokers will be as well fed and lodged as the captain or passengers; and the captain and the stoker will have the same pay.

There are plenty of enterprises which will be carried on then, as they are now (and, to be successful, must probably remain) under the guidance of one man. The only difference between then and now will be, that he will be chosen because he is fit for the work, and not because he must have a job found for him; and that he will do his work for the benefit of each and all, and not for the sake of making a profit. For the rest, time will teach us what new machinery may be necessary to the new life; reasonable men will submit to it without demur; and unreasonable ones will find themselves compelled to by the nature of things, and can only I fear console themselves, as the philosopher did when he knocked his head against the door post, by damning the Nature of things.

Well, since our aim is so great and so much to be longed for, the substituting throughout all society of peace for war, pleasure and self-respect for grief and disgrace, we may well seek about strenuously for some means for starting our enterprise; and since it is just these means in which the difficulty lies, I appeal to all socialists, while they express their thoughts and feelings about them honestly and fearlessly, not to make a quarrel of it with those whose aim is one with theirs, because there is a difference of opinion between them about the usefulness of the details of the means. It is difficult or even impossible not to make mistakes about these, driven as we are by the swift lapse of time and the necessity for doing something amidst it all. So let us forgive the mistakes that others make, even if we make none ourselves, and be at peace amongst ourselves, that we may the better make War upon the monopolist.

HOW I BECAME A SOCIALIST

[First published in *Justice*, June 16th, 1894. Cole, 655-59. In his last years Morris modified his long-held anti-Parliamentarian position, agreeing that the time had now come for the formation of a Socialist Party. He did not rejoin the S.D.F. but ended his breach with Hyndman to the extent of writing several articles for the S.D.F. journal, *Justice*. In this one he looks back over his life and sums up his development.]

I am asked by the Editor to give some sort of a history of the above conversion, and I feel that it may be of some use to do so, if my readers will look upon me as a type of a certain group of people, but not so easy to do clearly, briefly and truly. Let me, however, try. But first, I will say what I mean by being a Socialist, since I am told that the word no longer expresses definitely and with certainty what it did ten years ago. Well, what I mean by Socialism is a condition of society in which there should be neither rich nor poor, neither master nor master's man, neither idle nor overworked, neither brain-sick brain workers, nor heart-sick hand workers, in a word, in which all men would be living in equality of condition, and would manage their affairs unwastefully, and with the full consciousness that harm to one would mean harm to all—the realization at last of the meaning of the word COMMONWEALTH.

Now this view of Socialism which I hold to-day, and hope to die holding, is what I began with; I had no transitional period, unless you may call such a brief period of political radicalism during which I saw my ideal clear enough, but had no hope of any realization of it. That came to an end some months before I joined the (then) Democratic Federation, and the meaning of my joining that body was that I had conceived a hope of the realization of my ideal. If you ask me how much of a hope, or what I thought we Socialists then living and working would accomplish towards it, or when there would be effected any change in the face of society, I must say, I do not know. I can only say that I did not measure my hope, nor the joy that it brought me at the time. For the rest, when I took that step I was blankly ignorant of economics; I had never so much as opened Adam Smith, or heard of Ricardo, or of Karl Marx. Oddly enough, I *had* read some of Mill, to wit, those posthumous papers of his (published, was it in the *Westminster Review* or the *Fortnightly?*) in which he attacks Socialism in its Fourierist guise. In those papers he put the arguments, as far as they go, clearly and honestly, and the result, so far as I was concerned, was to convince me that Socialism was a necessary change, and that it was possible to bring it about in our own days. Those papers put the finishing touch to my conversion to Socialism. Well, having joined a Socialist body (for the Federation soon became definitely Socialist), I put some conscience into trying to learn the economical side of Socialism, and even tackled Marx, though I must confess that, whereas I thoroughly enjoyed the historical part of *Capital,* I suffered agonies of confusion of the brain over reading the pure economics of that great work. Anyhow, I read what I could, and will hope that some information stuck to me from my reading; but more, I must think, from continuous conversation with such friends as Bax and Hyndman and Scheu, and the brisk course of propaganda meetings which were going on at the time, and in which I took my share. Such finish to what of education in practical Socialism as I am capable of I received afterwards from some of my Anarchist friends, from whom I learned, quite against their intention, that Anarchism was impossible, much as I learned from Mill against *his* intention that Socialism was necessary.

But in this telling how I fell into *practical* Socialism I have begun, as I perceive, in the middle, for in my position of a well-to-do man, not suffering from the disabilities which oppress a working man at every step, I feel that I might never have been drawn into the practical side of the question if an ideal had not forced me to seek towards it. For politics as politics, i.e., not regarded as a necessary if cumbersome and disgustful means to an end, would never have attracted me, nor when I had become conscious of the wrongs of society as it now is, and the oppression of poor people, could I have ever believed in the possibility of a *partial* setting right of those wrongs. In other words, I could never have been such a fool as to believe in the happy and "respectable" poor.

If, therefore, my ideal forced me to look for practical Socialism, what was it that forced me to conceive of an ideal? Now, here comes in what I said of my being (in this paper) a type of a certain group of mind.

Before the uprising of *modern* Socialism almost all intelligent people either were, or professed themselves to be, quite contented with the civilization of this century. Again, almost all of these really were thus contented, and saw nothing to do but to perfect the said civilization by getting rid of a few ridiculous survivals of the barbarous ages. To be short, this was the *Whig* frame of mind, natural to the modern prosperous middle-class men, who, in fact, as far as mechanical progress is concerned, have nothing to ask for, if only Socialism would leave them alone to enjoy their plentiful style.

But besides these contented ones there were others who were not really contented, but had a vague sentiment of repulsion to the triumph of civilization, but were coerced into silence by the measureless power of Whiggery. Lastly, there were a few who were in open rebellion against the said Whiggery—a few, say two, Carlyle and Ruskin. The latter, before my days of practical Socialism, was my master towards the ideal aforesaid, and, looking backward, I cannot help saying, by the way, how deadly dull the world would have been twenty years ago but for Ruskin! It was through him that I learned to give form to my discontent, which I must say was not by any means vague. Apart from the desire to produce beautiful things, the leading passion of my life has been and is hatred of modern civilization. What shall I say of it now, when the words are put into my mouth, my hope of its destruction—what shall I say of its supplanting by Socialism?

What shall I say concerning its mastery of and its waste of mechanical power, its commonwealth so poor, its enemies of the commonwealth so rich, its stupendous organization—for the misery of life! Its contempt of simple pleasures which everyone could enjoy but for its folly? Its eyeless vulgarity which has destroyed art, the one certain solace of labour? All this I felt then as now, but I did not know why it was so. The hope of the past times was gone, the struggles of mankind for many ages had produced nothing but this sordid, aimless, ugly confusion; the immediate future seemed to me likely to intensify all the present evils by sweeping away the last survivals of the days before the dull squalor of civilization had settled down on the world. This was a bad look-out indeed, and, if I may mention myself as a personality and not as a mere type, especially so to a man of my disposition, careless of metaphysics and religion, as well as of scientific analysis, but with a deep love of the earth and the life on it, and a passion for the history of the past of mankind. Think of it! Was it all to end in a counting-house on the top of a cinder-heap, with Podsnap's drawing-room in the offing, and a Whig committee dealing out champagne to the rich and margarine to the poor in such convenient proportions as would make all men contented together, though the pleasure of the eyes was gone from the world, and the place of Homer was to be taken by Huxley? Yet, believe me, in my heart, when I really forced myself to look towards the future, that is what I saw in it, and, as far as I could tell, scarce anyone seemed to think it worth while to struggle against such a consummation of civilization. So there I was in for a fine pessimistic end of life, if it had not somehow dawned on me that amidst all this filth of civilization the seeds of a great change, what we others call Social-Revolution, were beginning to germinate. The whole face of things was changed to me by that discovery, and all I had to do then in order to become a Socialist was to hook myself on to the practical movement, which, as before said, I have tried to do as well as I could.

To sum up, then the study of history and the love and practice of art forced me into a hatred of the civilization which, if things were to stop as they are, would turn history into inconsequent nonsense, and make art a collection of the curiosities of the past, which would have no serious relation to the life of the present.

But the consciousness of revolution stirring amidst our hateful modern society prevented me, luckier than many others of artistic perceptions, from crystallizing into a mere railer against "progress" on the one hand, and on the other from wasting time and energy in any of the numerous schemes by which the quasi-artistic of the middle classes hope to make art grow when it has no longer any root, and thus I became a practical Socialist.

A last word or two. Perhaps some of our friends will say, what have we to do with these matters of history and art? We want by means of Social-Democracy to win a decent livelihood, we want in some sort to live, and that at once. Surely any one who professes to think that the question of art and cultivation must go before that of the knife and fork (and there are some who do propose that) does not understand what art means, or how that its roots must have a soil of a thriving and unanxious life. Yet it must be remembered that civilization has reduced the workman to such a skinny and pitiful existence, that he scarcely knows how to frame a desire for any life much better than that which he now endures perforce. It is the province of art to set the true ideal of a full and reasonable life before him, a life to which the perception and creation of beauty, the enjoyment of real pleasure that is, shall be felt to be as necessary to man as his daily bread, and that no man, and no set of men, can be deprived of this except by mere opposition, which should be resisted to the utmost.

THE WILLIAM MORRIS SOCIETY

The William Morris Society exists to promote a wider appreciation and deeper understanding of Morris, his friends and their work. The many-sidedness of Morris and the variety of activities in which he engaged bring together in this Society those who are interested in him as a poet, writer, designer, craftsman, printer, pioneer, socialist, dreamer, or who simply admire his robust and generous personality, his extraordinary vitality and his creative concentration.

The Society provides a meeting place for the large number of people who believe that Morris' work and ideals are of great value to the world of today. It has members in many different parts of the world and keeps in touch with these by means of newsletters, reprints of lectures and other publications. It arranges lectures, visits to places of interest and exhibitions. It encourages the publication of Morris' works and the continued manufacture of his textile and wallpaper designs. It enables those interested in Morris to become known to one another and fosters the exchange of ideas about him. The Journal of the Society is published twice a year. It is available only to members.